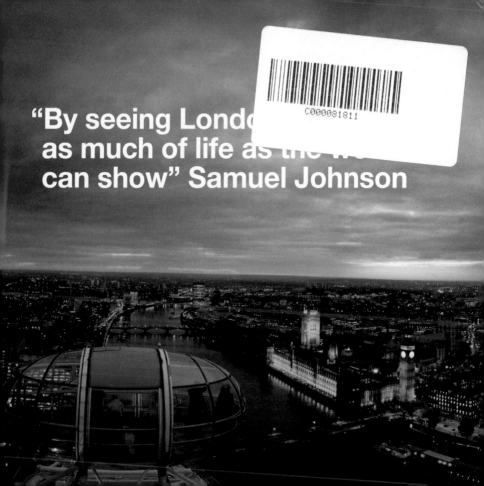

"By seeing Londo
as much of life as the wo
can show" Samuel Johnson

Did you know?

London is named after the ancient Roman settlement 'Londinium' built almost 2,000 years ago on the spot where the City of London now stands.

London covers a surface area of 611 square miles, that's 1,583 square kilometres and is made up of 32 boroughs and the City of London.

The town of Westminster became a city in 1540, when Henry VIII decided to make Westminster Abbey into a cathedral.

London is connected
to the rest of Great Britain
and Europe by 18 main-line
railway terminals and to the
rest of the world by three
international airports.

If you're driving to the capital, it's hard not to miss London's ring road, the London Orbital or M25, which opened in 1986.

It was the most expensive motorway ever built in Britain at the time. At 117 miles (188 kilometres), it's the largest orbital road of its kind in the world, used by over 200,000 vehicles each weekday (which sometimes turns it into the country's biggest car park).

The Dartford Tunnel opened in two phases, one tunnel in 1963 and the other in 1980. The Queen Elizabeth II Bridge was opened in 1991 by Her Majesty. During 2010 and 2011 over 50,940,000 vehicles used the Dartford crossings at a rate of up to 150,000 a day.

Towards the end of the 1980s and before the introduction of speed cameras, the M25 became the city's unofficial racetrack.

At night, many of the capital's supercar owners would meet at South Mimms service station and use the circular roadway for time trails. At an average speed of 117mph, some did the distance in under an hour (which included paying the toll at Dartford Tunnel!).

The longest time spent trying to get *off* the M25 belongs to a pensioner who found himself disoriented on the road while on his way to visit his daughter.

The trip, which should have only taken one hour, became a 48-hour nightmare. The gentleman was eventually found by police on the motorway's hard shoulder, 2 days after his family had reported him missing!

If you're taking to London on foot there are over 25,000 streets to explore, 4 UNESCO World Heritage Sites, that's the Tower of London, Maritime Greenwich, Westminster Palace and Kew's Royal Botanic Gardens.

Then we've got 40,000 listed buildings, 22 national museums, 200 or so other ones, 900 bookshops, 395 libraries, 105 cinemas and 40 theatres.

If you fancy a bit of retail therapy or are looking for something new for your wardrobe, the shops along Knightsbridge, Oxford Street and Regent Street are some of the largest and finest in the world.

If you want something a little more bespoke, 85% of the UK's fashion designers are based in London too!

If sport is your thing, London's home to some of the biggest sporting events and venues in the world and this year the British capital is hosting the 2012 Olympics and Paralympics.

If you like to get out and party, the city is home to some of Britain's top nightclubs and their resident DJs including the Ministry of Sound, Fabric, Heaven and Pacha. London's parks and other Large venues also host over 200 different festivals every year.

This year we celebrated the Queen's Diamond Jubilee and over the summer there'll be 10 million free opportunities to take part in events throughout the country and the capital as part of the London 2012 Festival.

Oh, and if you're wondering, while you're wandering through the many sights of London, where all those blue plaques come from, wonder no more.

The scheme was founded in 1866 by London's Royal Society of Arts and is the oldest of its kind in the world.

Across the city there are over 150,000 different plaques.

Today they are administered by the English Heritage office with the specific purpose of commemorating notable figures of London's past with the buildings where they lived or the place where they worked.

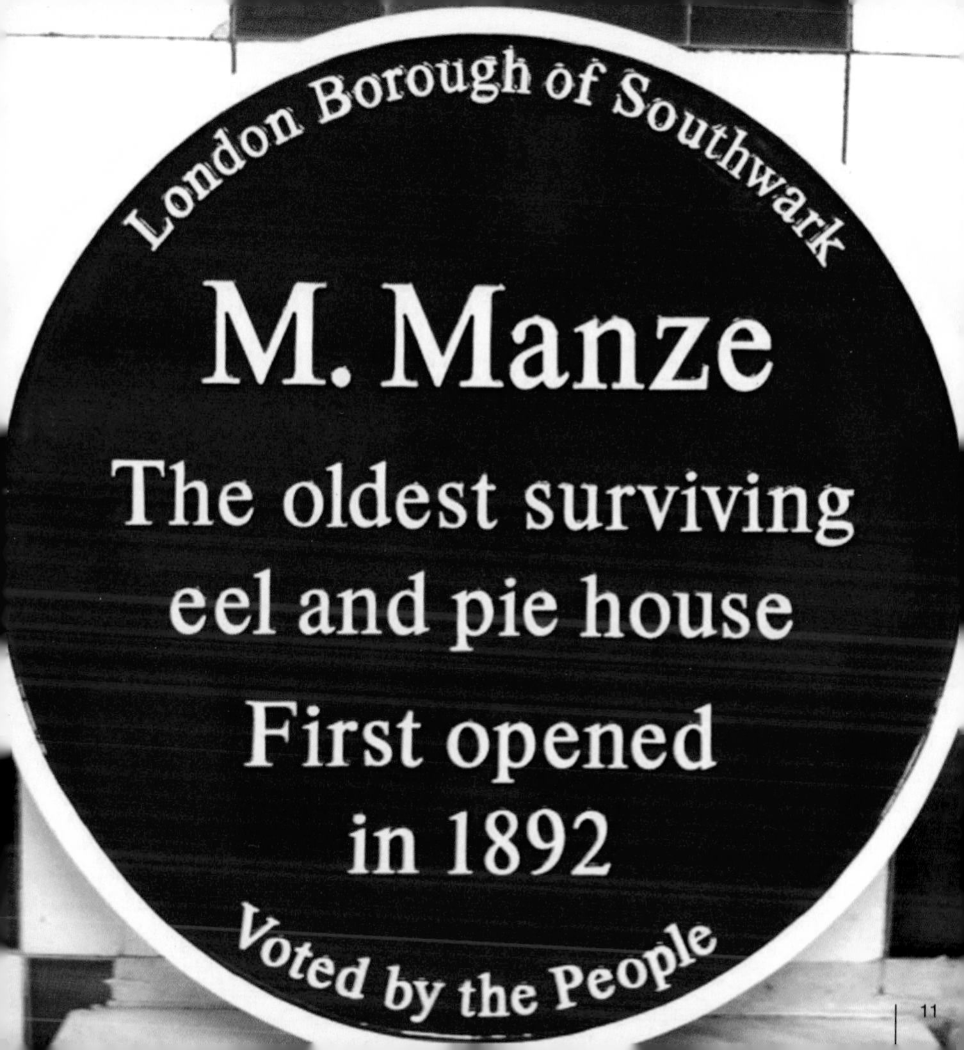

London Borough of Southwark

M. Manze

The oldest surviving
eel and pie house

First opened
in 1892

Voted by the People

If you've got this far, you'll realise this book is about London, which is without doubt one of the most vibrant and diverse cities in the world. It's big, it's colourful, it has an incredible heritage, it's the seat of the British monarchy and the British Government and home to millions of people from all over the world.

Its ancient financial district is one of the richest in the world and the capital's extensive range of creative, culinary and cultural offerings make London, indeed, a world within a city.

The extraordinary number of events and individuals that have shaped London's story are far too extensive for a little book so what we've tried to do here is give you a little, but wholesome, flavour of the place with an occasional dash of word play or humour. A lovely little read, with some fabulous photos that reflect the colourful and eclectic character of our beloved capital in a way that delights, celebrates and engages.

Just like our ever-growing little book collection, this isn't a travel guide but it does share information about places to explore and visit. It isn't a history book but it does delve into London's incredible past. This isn't a geographical account of the place but as you leaf through these pages, we hope you'll discover some interesting insights into London's many landmarks, extraordinary buildings and centres for culture and creativity (and there are lots of those).

Above all we hope this book is something that whets your appetite, an easy little read that offers up the story of London in bite-sized chunks, giving you a taste, if only a morsel, of London's phenomenal past and incredibly vibrant present.

London is the capital city of England and the United Kingdom (UK). Home to 12.5% of the UK's 61 million population, it's the most populated city in Western Europe.

With about 4,679 people per square mile, the UK's capital is the 18th largest metropolitan area in the world.

According to the City Mayor's Foundation, with more residents than nations like Denmark, New Zealand or the Republic of Ireland, it's the 23rd largest city on the planet!

In 1831, London was the first city in the world to reach a population of over one million residents.

For almost a century it remained the most densely populated city in the world. Then, in 1925, London fell into 2nd place after Tokyo, which, with a population of 32 million, is still the most populated city on the planet today.

The biggest drop in London's population took place during the 1660s when the city suffered the Great Plague, the last major epidemic to take place in the United Kingdom.

The Great Plague, also known as the Black Death after the colour of the lumps that appear on a victim's body, is believed to have come from the Netherlands. Despite banning any trade with the country, the first victims of the disease lived in London's docklands area, the first recorded victim being Rebecca Andrews on the 12th April 1665.

That year a hot summer escalated the death toll, so much so that London's nobility fled to the country and by June the city gates were closed to anyone without a certificate of health. Various records state that by July the death toll had reached 2,000 a week and at its peak in August, 7,000 a week.

A rumour that the disease was spread by dogs and cats led to the slaughter of over 40,000 dogs and some 200,000 cats (me-ouch).

The outbreak finally abated during the cold weather of the winter months. The following year's Great Fire of London was believed to have devastated and incinerated such large areas of the once infected city that the disease could never take hold again (more about that later).

It's estimated that the Great Plague of London claimed the lives of over 100,000 Londoners, 20% of the capital's population.

Today, the number of the capital's residents grows by the equivalent of a borough every two years. By 2016, it's estimated London will be home to more than eight million people.

In 2010, London's population stood at 7.83 million people, an increase of 71,600 on the previous year.

The London Councils organisation estimates that over 1.3 million people move in and out of London every year and an additional 1 million people enter the capital each weekday for work!

32% of Londoners belong to either black, Asian or other minority ethnic groups and 22.9 of the city's population are young people.

Just under 50% of today's Londoners are between 20 and 44 years old. 20% are under 16 years and just over 10% are of pension age or older.

These days if you live in London, if you are a man you can expect to live to about 77 years and if you're a woman you've got until about 82!

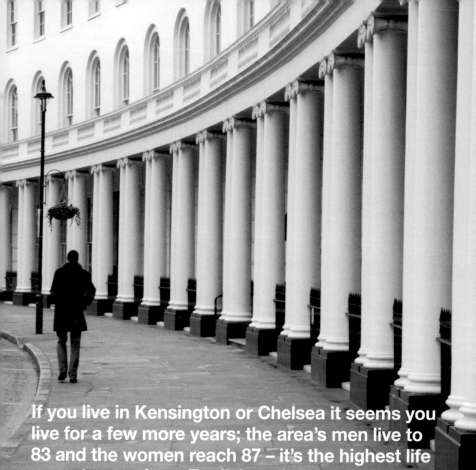

If you live in Kensington or Chelsea it seems you live for a few more years; the area's men live to 83 and the women reach 87 – it's the highest life expectancy of any English region.

Over 1.2 million of London's residents go to school.

Over 300 different languages are spoken across London's playgrounds, in some inner London areas fewer than half of the pupils have English as a first language.

Over 600,000 of London's children live below the poverty line, that's about 39% of the capital's children – by far the highest rate of children poverty of any region in Britain.

While London may be one of the richest capital's in the world, 4 in 10 of the city's children live in poverty.

Families living on the poverty line in London have a budget of £10 per person per day to buy what they need, for those outside the poverty trap it's an average of £44 per day. And while 15% of households in London have an income over £60,000, 22% of households bring home less than £15,000.

In 2010, 211 rough sleepers were counted across the streets of 15 London boroughs; ironically 147 of those were in Westminster, the richest!

In 1965 London was officially divided into 33 boroughs, which include the City of London, the oldest part of the capital and the City of Westminster, which is most of Central London and the West End.

The other Greater London boroughs are Barnet, Barking and Dagenham, Bexley, Brent, Bromley, Camden, Croydon, Ealing, Enfield, Greenwich, Hackney, Hammersmith and Fulham, Haringey, Harrow, Havering, Hillingdon, Hounslow, Islington, Kensington and Chelsea, Kingston upon Thames, Lambeth, Lewisham, Merton, Newham, Redbridge, Richmond upon Thames, Southwark, Sutton, Tower Hamlets, Waltham Forest and Wandsworth.

Each Greater London borough has its own council, which is led by the governance of the Greater London Authority (GLA) formed in 2000. The GLA is made up of the elected Mayor of London, 25 elected members of assembly and some 600 administrative staff.

In terms of space, the 58 square miles that make up Bromley, make it the largest borough in London, and it's the greenest – over half the borough consists of Green Belt countryside.

With a population of about 345,000 people, Croydon, London's southernmost borough, is the most populated borough and the City of London, with just 11,000 residents, is the least.

The City of Westminster is the wealthiest borough in London (well in England to be exact) **and the houses around the Kensington and Chelsea area are some of the most expensive pads on earth.**

Of the 23 million homes in England, 5 million are in London (43% of those are flats).

One of London's smallest properties is three-and-a-half-feet wide and was built across an alleyway. Today, it's part of the Tyburn Convent, No. 10 Hyde Park Place.

The other is a converted milliner's shop, wedged between two properties on Goldhawk Road, Shepherd's Bush. The five-storey dwelling has been converted to have two bedrooms and measures just 5 feet and 6 inches at its widest point.

One of London's thinnest houses, aptly named The Thin House, is shaped liked a wedge and can be found at the thin end of Thurloe Square, Knightsbridge.

One of London's greenest gaffs can be found within Container City, at Trinity Buoy Wharf.

First installed in 2001, architects at Urban Space Management have recycled old shipping containers and converted them into artists' studios and a number of apartments.

London's largest house and the Queen's official London residence is Buckingham Palace.

Set in a garden of 40 acres, Buckingham Palace has 775 rooms and employs a total of 800 staff. The accommodation includes 19 staterooms, 52 royal and guest bedrooms, 188 staff bedrooms and 78 bathrooms.

The house has 1,514 doors and 760 windows
(and, if you were wondering how many light bulbs it
takes to light the palace... they've counted... and it's
about 40,000 – I wonder who stands on the chair and
changes them?).

London's largest and most famous home, for animals that is, is Battersea Dogs and Cats Home.

The home, which began in 1860 as The Temporary Home for Lost and Starving Dogs was founded by Mrs Mary Tealby and based in Holloway. It moved to its current premises in 1871 and has been homing the capital's stray cats and dogs for 140 years since.

At any one time, Battersea Dogs and Cats Home is home to 450 dogs and 150 cats. Last year, across their now three centres, the organisation cared for **5,941 dogs and 2,963 cats** (and if you think you could care for one drop them a line, there is lots of information about re-homing animals on Battersea's website).

With some 7.8 million humans needing a home in London, it's no wonder that 7% or 200,000 of the capital's households are officially overcrowded (they're certainly overpriced).

According to the Office for National Statistics, 42% of Londoners rent their accommodation. Not surprising, seeing as the average London house price is £400,000 (which, for most of the capital, is between five and nine times the average wage).

So, if you're looking for something detached, look away now, unless you've got a spare £761,000 knocking around (and if that figure leaves you feeling flat, you'll need a good £350,000 to spend on one of those!).

According to Mercer's 2011 cost of living survey, London is the 18th most expensive city to live in on earth.

London's most expensive residential addresses include Parkside, Wimbledon Common where the average house price is £5 million and Mallard Street, just off Chelsea's King's Road where it's a mere £4 million.

In 2010, one of London's most expensive addresses, 1 Hyde Park, Westminster, sold for £136 million (which makes the issue of house prices in Cornwall pale into peanuts).

London's addresses were divided into postal districts (you know the ones – N, NW, SW, SE, W, WC, E and EC) **in 1856 by Sir Rowland Hill.**

N.W.3

Introduced in 1855, London's first postbox was green and stood at the corner of Fleet Street and Farringdon.

In 1874, the capital's postal cabinets were the first in England to be painted their famous crimson red. With thousands more to do across the country, it took the General Post Office (GPO) another decade to paint the rest!

London has been HQ for the Post Office since 1660, when Charles II began the Royal Mail.

London's first-ever postal sorting office opened on the site of an old prison in 1889 (for some it probably still is, especially at Christmas). By the turn of the century, the 7.5-acre Mount Pleasant site connected to the major London post offices via a 23-mile railway network, operated by the London Post Office Railway. By the turn of the 20th century, the depot handled all of London's incoming and outgoing mail. It was said to be the busiest sorting office in the world.

England's first-ever purpose-built post office and GPO headquarters opened in 1829 in St Martin's Le Grand. The building was demolished in 1910 but the site is now home to the headquarters of British Telecom (BT).

Formerly known as the Post Office Tower, the famous, purpose-built BT tower opened in 1961; at 177 metres it was the UK's tallest building of its day.

The tower was built to support the microwave aerials needed to carry telecommunications traffic between London and the rest of the UK (in the seventies all the cross country teams from London's universities also used it as a vertical training ground!).

Today, the BT tower is still a major communications hub for London and operates as the TV Network Switching Centre carrying all the relays and satellite signals for the capital's major broadcasting companies, including the BBC.

When the BBC began radio broadcasting in 1928, the first studio was at Savoy Hill, just off the Strand. Back then the building belonged to the Institute of Electrical Engineers, who rented accommodation to the BBC in 1923. Within five years, what began as two small studios had become nine and the ever-increasing demand for broadcast services required the BBC to move into more suitable premises.

When it came to television broadcasting, North London's Alexandra Palace became known worldwide as the birthplace for TV. The very first experimental broadcasts took place there during 1935.

When the BBC's Broadcasting House was built in 1932 it was the first purpose-built radio broadcast centre in the UK.

By the end of the millennium the building was in need of repair and, over the last seven years has been painstakingly redeveloped to deliver state-of-the-art digital broadcast facilities and the largest live newsroom in Europe.

By the time it's completed, Broadcasting House will be home to 5,500 staff operating 5 television studios, 9 radio networks and 3 x 24-hour news channels for over 285 million audience members worldwide!

When BBC Television Centre was built at Wood Lane, Shepherd's Bush in 1960, it was the world's first-ever purpose-built television production centre.

When it opened in 1925 at a cost of over £2 million, Bush House was believed to be the most expensive building in the world.

It became home of the BBC's foreign language broadcasting in 1941 after Broadcasting House, Portland Place had been bombed. For over 70 years, all of the BBC's foreign languages services have been based at Bush House even though the BBC has never owned the building.

Long before the days of global satellite communications, London's most iconic structure for communication has got to be the good old-fashioned call box.

Designed by Sir Giles Gilbert Scott in 1924, the first prototype of London's famous red telephone boxes can be found at the entrance of The Royal Academy (he did some bigger stuff too which we'll come on to).

London's red phone boxes came about as part of a design competition organised by the Royal Fine Art Commission. Sir Gilbert Scott's creation, which became the K2 design, had 18 panes of glass on three of the sides and was made of cast iron (there's about 200 of them left across London today).

London's blue call boxes were installed across the capital between 1928 and 1937. They belonged to the police force and connected to the local police station.

London's police call boxes were special in that they had a blue light on top. When it flashed, it signalled to the local bobby to call his nearest station. (The Tardis, the most famous police call box in the world however, is connected to the rest of the universe).

Today, while London's police force no longer uses its phone boxes, it spends much of its time dealing with phone crime.

According to the Metropolitan Police, every month over 10,000 mobiles phones are stolen throughout Greater London.

Lost or stolen mobiles account for 45% of reported crimes on the Underground.

In the year since April 2011, Transport for London's Lost Property Office (LPO) has collected over 20,000 lost mobiles, approximately 36,000 books, 28,000 bags and 27,000 items of clothing. They've over £250,000 worth of luxury watches too – not to mention the laptops and iPads.

During the 1960s, the most regularly lost item on the capital's transport service was the umbrella. Back then they'd log over 90,000 brollies a year, today they recover just 7,000 (is it raining less?).

In 2009, Transport for London's LPO celebrated its 75th birthday. Based at Baker Street, with its famous fictional neighbour Sherlock Holmes, the LPO's computer system, which catalogues all the lost items, has been named after him!

With over 7.5 decades of logging London's lost items, some great things have been found: a samurai sword, a stuffed puffer fish, a prosthetic arm, a human skull, some breast implants, a lawnmower, a home vasectomy kit and a coffin (bet that was a dead loss!).

If you're looking to find things in London (rather than lose them)**, then cop hold of a copy of the A-Z. It's the most famous street map in the world.**

Created and researched by Phyllis Pearsall in 1935, the first A-Z street map of London went by the name of the A-Z Atlas and Guide to London (you can still get copies of it).

The inspiration to collate the city's first street map came after Pearsall spent a rainy night lost and on foot in London while trying to find the location of a Belgravia dinner party. Hours late and after being let down by an old Ordnance Survey map, she arrived at the party having resolved to rewrite the walking routes of London.

Throughout the late 1930s, Phyllis Pearsall painstakingly worked 18-hour days, walking a total of 3,000 miles as she mapped each and every one of London's 23,000 streets.

With the help of just one draughtsman, James Duncan, Pearsall completed the first edition towards the end of the decade. With investment from her father, Pearsall decided to publish the book on her own. The first print-run was for 10,000 maps and the first-ever A-Z Atlas and Guide to London was an instant success.

Colches
87
Chelmsford
LONDON
Sou
ldock 65
chop's
ortford
t Albans
25
37
Tilbury
Tham
Rochester
15
83
17
13
15
Mai
Staines
20

Today there are 25,000 streets listed in the A-Z. Here are a few of them:

One of the healthiest streets in London is Harley Street.

Developed in 1820, Harley Street was originally most famous for its artists, Allan Ramsay lived at No. 67 and J.M.W. Turner lived at No. 64. Today almost every residential address houses either a clinic or surgery and the area is home to 1,500 physicians and 8 private hospitals.

London's Great Ormond Street is home to the world's most famous children's hospital.

At a time when a third of London's children were dying before adulthood, the Great Ormond Street Hospital for Sick Children opened on St Valentine's Day in 1852, with just 10 beds.

Founded by Dr Charles West it was the only hospital in Britain to offer in-patient care to children only. It very quickly attracted support, most famously from J M Barrie, author of *Peter Pan*, who after taking the cast of his London show to perform especially at the hospital's nursery, became a significant financial donor.

From 1929 onwards, Barrie donated all the royalties from *Peter Pan* to the hospital. This meant that up until 2007, whenever *Peter Pan* was staged or a book published, a percentage of the ticket or book price was paid to Great Ormond Street.

Today, Great Ormond Street has 900 nurses, 29 wards, 335 beds and the hospital treats over 99,000 children a year.

221B Baker Street is the famous home of Sir Arthur Conan Doyle's character Sherlock Holmes.

Not only is Baker Street, the fictional address of one of the world's most famous detectives, but in 1835 Baker Street became home to London's first exhibition of Madame Tussaud's Wax Works.

Madame Tussaud's opened over 200 years ago, since then millions of visitors have got up close and personal with life-sized wax impressions of the world's celebrities, politicians, sporting heroes and notable figures from history.

Madame Tussaud learned her trade to model wax in France under the guidance of her tutor Dr Phillipe Curtis. After a failed marriage she came to Britain in 1802 bringing with her some of her finest figures, which she exhibited in London.

In 1835 she moved to Baker Street where her work found a permanent London exhibition in the Baker Street Bazaar. There, people paid sixpence to see her waxworks of the biggest names of the day. In 1884 her son moved the exhibition to Marylebone Road, where it still stands today.

Madame Tussaud died in 1850 but her work and exhibitions continued with the business being passed down through a number of generations.

Today the attraction is owned by Merlin Entertainment Group and Madame Tussaud's wax museums can be experienced in Hollywood, Hong Kong, Bangkok and Sydney.

With over 150 years of experience each figure takes four months and 20 sculptors to create and costs about £150,000. Over 500 precise face and body measurements have to be taken with the subject sitting for at least 2 hours. Once the wax figure has been sculpted, every single real hair is inserted individually (because they're worth it!).

London's most fashionable address is Carnaby Street. During the 1960s, the area's boutiques led the way in London's fashion scene and Carnaby Street was the world capital of cool.

Carnaby's first clothing shop His Clothes opened in 1957 by fashion designer John Stephens. Within a few years it had become a Mecca for all kinds of boutiques featuring the work of some of Britain's most influential fashion designers.

London's Fashion Week is the highlight of the British fashion industry's calendar. Last year hundreds of buyers came from 13 different countries placing orders from Britain worth over £74,120,000!

London's King's Road, which stretches through Chelsea and Fulham was once home to the Glaciarium, the world's first artificially frozen ice rink.

In the 1960s the likes of fashion designers Vivienne Westwood and Mary Quant gave the King's Road a very different kind of cool and even today it's regarded as the place to go shopping. In 1999, the road became home to Britain's very first Starbucks.

Notting Hill's Portobello Road has one of the largest and most famous antiques markets in the world.

Although the street name was removed in 1846, Petticoat Lane (now Middlesex Street) **was, and still is, home to one of the world's most famous Sunday street markets.**

London's Abbey Road in St John's Wood, home to the first Abbey National Building Society and the famous EMI studios, rose to fame in 1969 when The Beatles named their final LP after it.

The studios, owned by the Gramophone Company, opened at No. 3 Abbey Road, Westminster, in 1931. EMI officially changed the name to the Abbey Road Studios in 1970. Since then, Abbey Road has been synonymous with the best of British music including Cliff Richard and the Shadows, The Beatles, The Hollies, Pink Floyd, Adam Ant, Duran Duran and more recently Radiohead, Travis and Leona Lewis.

Downing Street was built between 1682 and 1684 by George Downing.

Downing was so tight that when building his cul-de-sac of investment properties instead of laying a neat brick facade he had mortar lines drawn (yes drawn) onto the exterior of the building to give the impression of evenly-spaced bricks! Winston Churchill described the premises as "shaky and lightly built by the profiteering contractor whose name they bear".

Today, 10 Downing Street is home to the British Prime Minister, his family and Larry the cat, from Battersea Dogs and Cats Home, who works as chief mouser.

London's Fleet Street is named after the River Fleet, one of London's lost rivers, which runs beneath it.

Mayfair was named after the fortnightly May Fair, which took place between 1686 and 1764 in what is now one of Mayfair's small squares called Shepherd Market. Westminster's Park Lane and Mayfair owe much of their notoriety to the American-invented game Monopoly of which the London edition arrived in the capital in 1936.

Piccadilly takes its name from a 17th-century tailor who sold picadels, the big frilly collars worn by heads of state and notable people, often depicted in portraits.

Piccadilly is famously home to Fortnum and Mason, the Queen's favourite grocery store, which has been known for selling exquisite food and drink items since it was founded by William Fortnum and Hugh Mason in 1707.

While Mason was an experienced store holder, Fortnum an ex-employee of the royal family had an eye for quality products that would attract the bourgeoisie. Together they created one of the most lavish grocery stores on earth.

Today, Fortnum and Mason is famous the world over for its hampers, which in their 300-year history are probably the oldest and best-travelled tuck boxes on the planet.

The Piccadilly store ships 120,000 hampers worldwide each year and is still one of the most refined places to go food shopping, complete with 3 restaurants, a tea room and champagne bar.

Regent Street was designed by one of London's most famous Regency architects John Nash and named after the Prince Regent, who became George IV.

With over 2 kilometres of shop frontages, Regent Street attracts more than 7.5 million shoppers a year. Each building is listed and some are home to Britain's oldest retailers.

In 1875, with three staff and a loan of £2,000 from his father-in-law, Arthur Lasenby Liberty leased half a shop at 218a Regent Street.

By 1885, known for its exotic imports and luxurious fabrics and furnishings, Liberty had become the most fashionable place to shop in London. Today, the emporium remains one of London's leading retail destinations.

Hamleys is the largest toyshop in the world. Founded by Cornishman William Hamley in 1760, the Regent Street premises were opened in 1881 by his grandson.

Today Hamleys department store has over 5,000 square metres of retail space, entirely dedicated to toys and games and the art of play.

As well as being famous for its Christmas lights, London's Oxford Street's 300 stores make it the busiest road of high street retailers in Europe.

Some 200 million people are believed to visit the street every year. Last Christmas, Oxford Street retailers were taking a total of £1.5 million every ten minutes.

Running two kilometres from Marble Arch to St Giles Circus, Oxford Street is named after the Earl of Oxford who, during the 18th century, acquired most of the land in order to develop it. 200 years on and retailers regard their Oxford Street branch as their flagship UK store.

Oxford Street's HMV is the largest music store in Europe.

HMV is named after a painting of a dog listening to a phonograph created in 1899 by Francis Barraud entitled His Masters Voice. When the image became the logo of HMV, the phonograph was changed to the gramophone, still in use as the logo today.

House of Fraser opened in 1935. It was the first department store in Britain to install an escalator between every floor!

John Lewis opened its Oxford Street doors in 1864. Today, it's the third largest department store in Britain.

Marks and Spencer's Marble Arch has over 16,000 square metres of retail space making it the largest branch in the company.

Selfridges, the second largest department store in Britain, was founded by Harry Gordon Selfridge and opened on in 1909. Today, the store's beauty hall is the largest in the world selling 7,700 lipsticks, 2,800 mascaras and 1,000 bottles of nail polish a week!

The Knightsbridge home of Harvey Nichols opened in 1880, before that founder Benjamin Harvey opened his first linen store in 1813 on the corner of Knightsbridge and Sloane Square.

At No. 2 Hans Road, just off Knightsbridge, you'll find Rigby and Peller, a family business, which began in 1977. Owner June Kenton and her husband Harold have been in the corsetry trade for over 40 years.

With an extensive client list including members of the royal family and a wide range of celebrities, Rigby and Peller has held the Royal Warrant of Appointment of Corsetieres to HM Queen Elizabeth since 1960 (in short, it's one of the finest places in Britain to have a proper fitting and buy a lovely bra!).

Harrods is named after Henry Harrod, a tea merchant who bought a store in Knightsbridge in 1849.

Today, the five-acre site of Harrods, London's largest department store, boasts over one million square feet of retail space. With 330 different departments, 32 restaurants and some 5,000 staff it is the biggest in Britain. Sold by Mohamed Al-Fayed in 2010 for a mere £1.5 billion, during peak periods, it welcomes over 300,000 shoppers a day.

At night, Harrods' famous exterior lighting display is illuminated by over 11,500 light bulbs (imagine the electricity bill).

London's Battersea Power Station supplied London with electricity for over 50 years.

Battersea Power Station, designed by Sir Giles Gilbert Scott, the same chap who designed London's red phone boxes and the now Tate Modern, was a coal-fired operation made up of two stations. Station A started generating electricity in 1933 and station B fired up in 1955.

At that time Battersea Power Station was providing London with a fifth of its electricity. Due to rising operating costs and reduced energy production, station A closed in 1975 and B shut down in 1983.

Today, while Battersea Power Station may no longer fire up coal for electricity, the buildings are now listed and its architecture lights a spark in the hearts of numerous Londoners. For some it's the landmark building of the capital.

Despite a number of attempts to redevelop the site, in February 2012, Battersea Power Station went onto the commercial property market for £500 million (and that really would burn a hole in your pocket).

In 2010, London's electricity bill came to over £12 billion, that's a total of 151,903 GWh, 151,903,000,000,000 watts of power.

That same year, the capital's water consumption splashed in at a total of 444,205,000,000 litres! Keeping the capital clean and watered requires some 1,217 million litres of H_2O every 24 hours.

In 2010, around 26% of London's total water consumption was lost in leakages. Thames Water, who looks after 30,000 of London's mains water pipes, has a hell of a job trying to catch the drips. No wonder, a third of London's mains water pipes are over 150 years old.

In Victorian times the waste from overflowing cesspits contaminated London's water supply with all manner of infectious diseases including cholera. Back then doctors didn't know that water could carry bacteria and spread disease.

On 31st August 1854, the outbreak and spread of cholera from Soho's Broad Street Pump was about to change history, leading to one of the world's most significant discoveries in public health.

Up until Victorian times, the spread of disease was explained by the miasma theory, which held that cholera, chlamydia or the plague were caused by a miasma, a Greek word for pollution, which in Britain meant a noxious form of bad air!

Fortunately, the London physician, Dr John Snow thought this theory was a load of hot air and, on talking to the families of the Soho cholera victims, he put together a spot map, which marked out how the outbreak centred on the Broad Street Pump.

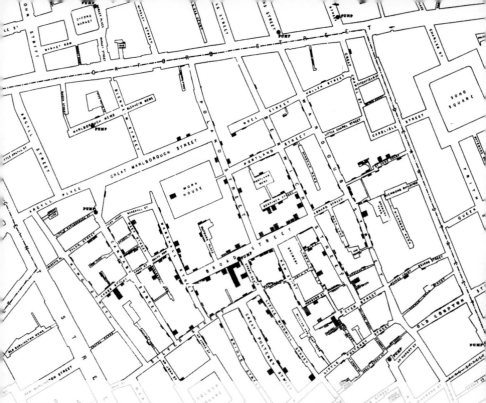

When cholera was affecting 12% of the population, Snow's discovery was one of the most significant public health discoveries of his time. Today, it's regarded as the founding event of the science of epidemiology, the study of how diseases spread.

Every year, flushing London's loos creates a staggering 32 million cubic metres of excess waste, which gets flushed into the Thames by rainwater. (That's enough poo and pee to fill the O2 stadium 15 times over, imagine the smell).

Alongside Snow's discovery of water-borne diseases, London's smelliest period in history gave birth to the sewerage system the capital still uses today.

Up until the 19th century, the River Thames was the capital's cesspit and dumping ground for the dead. All kinds of excrement, human and animal, ended up in the river as well as the bodies of dead dogs, cats, livestock and horses (not to mention the humans).

During the sweltering summer of 1858, decaying carcasses and floating faeces travelling down the Thames caused a stench so revolting that it closed parliament and became known ever after as "The Big Stink".

Within months the government had commissioned Joseph Bazalgette, an engineer of the newly formed Metropolitan Board of Works, to design a brand new network of sewers, which would carry the waste away from the city and out to the sea.

London's 83-mile long sewerage system, built over 160 years ago, took nearly a decade to complete.

The construction, which required the removal of 2.5 million cubic metres of earth and the laying of over 318 million bricks, created 83 miles of main sewers and a further 1,100 miles of street sewers, most of which are still in use today.

With so many people living in London, in whatever form it comes, waste management is critical to public health, making it a crucial public service.

We often forget that our lovely planet is a closed system (apart from satellites, spaceships and astronauts), **sunlight is the only thing that enters and leaves the earth's atmosphere.** So, when it comes to the waste we produce, there's no such place as away.

Even when we say we're throwing something away, that away just means somewhere else and for London, like everywhere else, that somewhere else is landfill.

London has 18 landfill sites, the largest of which is Mucking Marshes, in the Essex hamlet of Mucking. It's one of the largest landfill sites in Europe.

London's waste travels to Mucking, which is just 30 miles downstream of Tower Bridge, in hundreds of yellow containers. At Mucking wharf the waste containers are uploaded onto trucks and then unloaded onto the site's waste tips.

London's landfill sites will be full by 2025. Not surprising if over 1 million tonnes of London's food waste ends up in landfill and 0.5 million tonnes of the capital's waste wood isn't recycled (that really is rubbish!).

Every year London produces over 22 million tonnes of waste. 19% comes from households, 34% comes from offices and factories and the rest (47%) comes from the capital's construction and demolition works.

In 2010, household recycling efforts saved the capital £30 million. At the moment London's recycling rate is just 21% when over 60% of what Londoners throw away could be.

London's most famous recyclers are The Wombles, created by Elisabeth Beresford in 1968.

The stories were so popular that in 1973 the BBC decided to make a stop-motion animation series about the characters.

The Wombles, who are said to live for some 200 years, lived in burrows on Wimbledon Common. They were known for collecting and reusing rubbish in all manner of inventive ways (London's first recyclers, wonder if they're still there).

London's most famous bear started his journey in London when he was purchased from Selfridges on Christmas Eve 1956.

Michael Bond bought the bear as a Christmas gift for his wife and they decided to call him Paddington, after where they lived. Within two years Paddington's first story had been written and published by William Collins (now Harper Collins).

The first Paddington Bear toy arrived in 1972 as a Christmas present for, believe it or not, Jeremy Clarkson! His mum and dad set up a business making them.

In 2012, Paddington Bear was officially named as Britain's favourite ever animated character.

PLATFO

Paddington Station is one of 18 main-line "London Terminals" which include Blackfriars, Cannon Street, Charing Cross, City Thameslink, Euston, Fenchurch Street, King's Cross, Liverpool Street, London Bridge, Marylebone, Moorgate, Old Street, St Pancras International, Vauxhall, Victoria, Waterloo and Waterloo East.

London Paddington was the London terminus for the famous Great Western Railway. Most of today's station buildings date back to 1854 and were designed by Isambard Kingdom Brunel.

RM 9¾

London King's Cross opened in 1852. Today, it's most famous for being home to platform 9¾, the secret platform for any wizards wishing to travel on Harry Potter's Hogwarts Express.

The new concourse, which opened in March 2012, will enable the station to double the number of passengers it handles every year to over 48 million people (the statistics on witches and wizards haven't been published yet!).

London Euston, which opened in 1837, greets over 30 million passengers each year (and no wizards as far we know). It's the capital's 6th busiest station connecting London to Ireland, Scotland and Wales via destinations throughout the West Midlands, the north-west and North Wales.

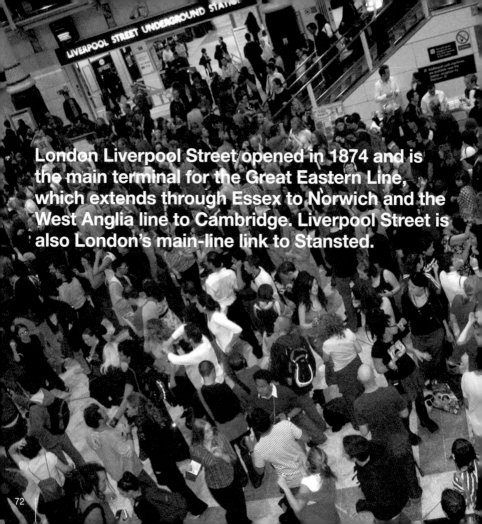

London Liverpool Street opened in 1874 and is the main terminal for the Great Eastern Line, which extends through Essex to Norwich and the West Anglia line to Cambridge. Liverpool Street is also London's main-line link to Stansted.

Liverpool Street's busiest moment came in February 2009 when 13,000 dancers took to the concourse in a true flash-mob response to the flash-mob style t-mobile advert that had been filmed at the station in January. At 7pm, police closed the station for 90 minutes as people from all over the UK took part in their own private disco.

London Victoria, greets over 70 million passengers a year. It's had a fair few flash mobs in its time and a few flash floods, caused by rain overflowing from the roof, which shut the station in July 2007 and July 2009 (that's the British summer for you).

London Victoria connects to the London Underground, Gatwick Airport and Victoria coach station making it the busiest long-distance travel interchange terminal in London. The station connects London to the south and south-east including Brighton, Hove, Canterbury and Dover.

Victoria tube station, which is in the process of a £700 million redevelopment, connects to the Victoria, Circle and District lines. It's the second busiest station on the London Underground.

London Waterloo, which opened in 1848, greets over 88 million passengers a year. In terms of through-put it's the busiest station in Great Britain.

London's busiest airport is Heathrow.

In 2011, more than 68 million people landed at London Heathrow making it the busiest airport in Europe and the third busiest in the world. Staff numbers alone total 75,000 people.

In 1930, Heathrow, or London Airport as it was known then, was a single grass strip, today its two runways total 7.5 kilometres of tarmac landing over 480,000 planes a year. The airport's five terminals are home to 86 airlines flying to 183 different countries.

London Gatwick is based in Sussex, about 32 miles south of Central London. The airport was developed from 1952 as an alternative to Heathrow.

The new £7 million complex, which was opened by HM The Queen on 9th June 1958, was the world's first airport accessible by all modes of transport; air, rail and road.

In its first year Gatwick carried 186,000 passengers. Today 32 million people arrive or depart from the airport.

London Gatwick is home to 90 airlines, which fly to over 200 destinations. The Gatwick Express, which terminates at Victoria, makes the airport just 30 minutes from London.

Today, over 75% of visitors to Britain come through one of London's airports.

Every year, some 14 million visitors arrive in London. That's a total sleepover of over 26 million nights.

In 2010, London's tourist economy contributed over £3 billion to the capital's coffers. The industry supports 13% of London's workforce, that's over 260,000 jobs.

With over 100,000 hotel rooms available, London is said to be the third most internationally visited city on earth.

London's hotel industry boomed during the 1800s alongside the development and completion of Britain's great railways.

London's first large-scale hotels were built by the railway companies, which were situated (as many still are today) **above or next to a number of London's main-line stations.**

Before the introduction of rail travel and the subsequent development of London's hotel and tourist industry, visitors to London arrived by stagecoach taking accommodation at coaching inns, some rented lodgings and wealthy country landowners rented houses.

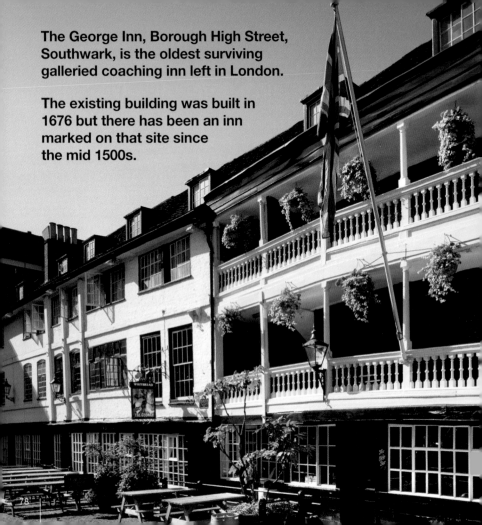

The George Inn, Borough High Street, Southwark, is the oldest surviving galleried coaching inn left in London.

The existing building was built in 1676 but there has been an inn marked on that site since the mid 1500s.

Today the George Inn runs as a pub and is owned by the National Trust.

The Tabard, London's most famous inn, was first built in 1307 and would have stood next door to the George Inn.

The Tabard was originally constructed as a hostel for the Abbot of Hyde who needed somewhere for him and his brethren to stay while in London. He also required a place where he could accommodate the many pilgrims who were making their annual trip to Canterbury Cathedral and the shrine of Thomas Becket.

While the Tabard no longer stands, the inn and its landlord Harry Bailey have been immortalised in Geoffrey Chaucer's *Canterbury Tales*.

When it was opened in 1865 by the Prince of Wales, The Langham Hotel was London's largest and Europe's grandest hotel.

Famous guests include Sir Arthur Conan Doyle, George Orwell, Mark Twain and Oscar Wilde. The hotel was bombed during the Second World War and legend has it that a German ghost haunts one of the corridors (and if that doesn't lift your spirits it was the first building in England to use hydraulic lifts).

When The Savoy opened its doors in 1889, it was the first hotel in London to have en-suite bathrooms in every room.

Savoy Court is the only street in the UK where vehicles have to drive on the right. This is because during the days of the hackney carriages, the passenger doors opened backwards so the driver could open the door from his window, without getting out of the cab.

In 2007, The Savoy closed for the first time in its 118-year history. The buildings were scheduled for a 15-month restoration project at an estimated cost of £100 million. On 10th October 2010, after a total cost of £220 million, The Savoy opened its doors once again and its first guest, who pulled up in the hotel's very own Rolls-Royce Phantom, was actor, broadcaster and writer Stephen Fry. The building was officially opened in November by HRH Prince Charles.

Today The Savoy still retains its position as one of the world's finest hotels.

Claridge's, London's art-deco jewel, was first known as The Mivert, a high-class hotel that took up five houses along London's Mayfair. In 1854, The Mivert was bought by Mr and Mrs Claridge, who renamed it Claridge's, Late Mivert's.

By 1860, Claridge's had its own similarly excellent reputation, which was confirmed when Queen Victoria and Prince Albert arrived on a visit to see Empress Eugenie of France, who'd made Claridge's her winter HQ (imagine it).

During the Second World War the hotel became a royal refuge giving safe-haven to the Kings of Greece, Norway and Yugoslavia and the Queen of the Netherlands (quite some air-raid shelter).

In 1947, a diplomat is said to have called Claridge's asking to speak to the King. "Certainly sir," came the polite response.

Loved by the royals, Claridge's has also been adored and adorned with Hollywood stars – Audrey Hepburn, Cary Grant and Bing Crosby have strolled through Claridge's lobby. Katharine Hepburn, however, had to use the staff entrance. She was barred from the lobby because she insisted on wearing trousers, which contravened the strict dress code of the time.

In 2011, The Dorchester celebrated its 80th Anniversary. The hotel, which opened in 1931, was designed by Sir Malcolm McAlpine and Sir Francis Towles who wanted to create "the perfect hotel".

During the Second World War, The Dorchester became a central meeting place. Because of its modern architecture the building was regarded to be one of the safest during wartime London.

Over its 80 years of service, The Dorchester has been no stranger to celebrities welcoming all kinds of stars including Noel Coward, Louis Armstrong, Tom Cruise, Johnny Depp, Britney Spears and Lady Gaga.

In 1947, it was where Prince Phillip held his "stag night". In 1966 it was the place where Elizabeth Taylor accepted her contract to star as Cleopatra and in 1974, Al Pacino dropped in booking a Dorchester suite for the press launch of Godfather Part II.

The Grosvenor, Park Lane, was the former residence of the Duke of Westminster. Today, it has the largest number of four-star rooms in London.

The Grosvenor opened just over 150 years ago. On top of its 494 bedrooms, it's home to one of the largest ballrooms in Europe. The Great Room, which can accommodate some 2,000 diners (imagine the size of the kitchen), was originally built as an ice rink!

One of the most expensive places to stay in London is The Lanesborough, Knightsbridge.

Before it was renovated into a hotel, the Lanesborough building was St George's Hospital, the workplace of Florence Nightingale, the world's most famous nurse.

Today, the hotel and its 93 rooms, which include 43 suites has been painstakingly restored to one of the finest examples of a 19th-century London residence. So much so that when you stay, you even get your own butler.

The Ritz opened in 1906. Over the last century, Tea at Ritz has become a bit of an institution.

The Palm Court at The Ritz is famous for its afternoon tea, which is served daily over five sittings and includes sandwiches, scones and delightful patisseries (reservations are essential and no jeans or trainers!).

During the 1920s, The Waldorf Hotel was one of the first places in London to hold Latin-style ballroom dance classes. The hotel quickly became synonymous with tea dances, which continued weekly, sometimes daily, up until its dance hall was bombed at the beginning of the Second World War.

The Waldorf Hotel, today the Waldorf Hilton, opened in 1908, in Aldwych, the heart of London's theatreland.

In 1982, the hotel re-introduced its tea dance programme, which still continues on **Sunday afternoons** (but check before you go). With most of London's top hotels now offering an exquisite menu for afternoon tea, it's a wonder anyone's got room for supper. If you do you'll also be spoilt for choice.

London's home to 6,000 different restaurants, that's 16% of the UK's eateries.

The Great British capital can also boast over 70 Michelin star restaurants and gastro-pubs, 36 of which can be found in the City of Westminster (yum).

Eating out in London is worth over £1.6 billion to the capital's economy and you can choose from a menu of over 50 different cuisines.

London's oldest restaurant, Simpson's Tavern was founded in 1757.

Proprietor Thomas Simpson began his career in cooking in 1753 by opening his Fish Ordinary Restaurant in Bell Alley, near Billingsgate Fish Market. His customers were mainly market workers who'd bring Simpson fish, which he'd prepare and cook for them.

Thomas Simpson moved his business into the city in 1757 where, at Ball Court, 38½ Corn Hill, the tavern is still situated today. Even though the menu has been modernised, the venue hasn't changed since the 1800s. Complete with old-fashioned style stalls, the interior has retained all the character of a 19th-century London chophouse.

Westminster's oldest restaurant Rules opened in Covent Garden in 1798.

Two centuries on and three families later, Rules is owned by John Mayhew, who also owns the Lartington Estate in the High Pennines.

The 200-year-old restaurant has always been famous for serving traditional British food and specialises in classic game cookery, which it sources from its Lartington Estate, as well as oysters, pies and good old-fashioned British puddings!

Simpson's-in-the-Strand opened in 1828 as a chess and coffee house and after attracting Howard Stauton, the first English chess champion through its doors, the restaurant soon became the "home of chess".

Other famous clientele have included Vincent Van Gogh, Charles Dickens and George Bernard Shaw. Today Simpson's-in-the-Strand is also famed for serving classic British dishes in exquisite surroundings.

Before Kettner's opened in 1867 it was a row of four Georgian Houses.

Auguste Kettner, chef to Napoleon III, was a renowned host with a reputation for holding incredible parties. His guests included Agatha Christie, Bing Crosby, Edward VII and Oscar Wilde. Today, Kettner's 1930's style restaurant and champagne bar is situated in Soho, a top spot for pre- and post-theatre dining.

London's first fish and chip shop is believed to have been opened in 1860 in Cleveland Street by Joseph Malin (while chipping away at the research for this book, we discovered that some believe Mr Malin was Jewish and some say he's Cornish. Whatever his origin he's certainly earned his plaice in history!).

Set in the heart of the City of London, Sweetings is based on the corner of Queen Victoria Street, a traditional Victorian fish and oyster bar.

Today, you'll find a traditionally simple "bill of fare", which includes potted shrimp, native oysters from the West Mersea coast of Essex, lobster and crab bisque and good old-fashioned smoked eel.

The traditional dish of jellied eels originated during the 18th century in London's East End (well someone had to do it).

The dish is prepared by cooking chopped eel in a spicy stock, which as it cools forms its own jelly. During the 1700s this was the food of the poor, today it's seen as a bit of a delicacy with just a few traditional eel, pie and mash places left in London.

87 Tower Bridge Road SE1 is home to the oldest pie and mash shop in London.

The business, which was originally founded by Robert Cook in 1891, was taken over by Michele Manze in 1902. The Manze family were originally from Ravello in Southern Italy and moved to Bermondsey where they began selling ice cream. By 1930, Michele and his brothers owned 14 pie and mash shops.

Today, three generations on, the Manze family still own and run a number of pie and mash shops, one at Tower Bridge, one at 105 High Street, Peckham and another at 226 High Street, Sutton – and you can order an eel, pie and mash pack from their website (caught on line, bought on line - see back for details!).

If you just fancy a quick pint, there are over 3,000 pubs in London and the capital's home to some of the largest and oldest breweries in Britain.

The Young & Co. Brewery dates back to 1831 when Charles Young and Anthony Bainbridge bought the Ram Brewery, Wandsworth.

With a history of brewing on the Wandsworth site dating back to the 1570s, until it closed on the 25th September 2006, Young's Brewery was the oldest in Britain.

The Young's Brewery was famously home to a number of animals, which included a ram, some geese and a dozen horses. Young's brewery still used the traditional horse-drawn drays to deliver beer to local pubs right up until it closed.

Today Young's runs over 220 pubs in London and Somerset and its beer is brewed at the Eagle Brewery, Bedford.

The Fullers Brewery, Chiswick, is most famous for its London Pride and HSB.

The Chiswick site, on the Hogarth roundabout, at the end of the M4 has been brewing beer for 350 years. Today the company has over 360 pubs on its books (people drank a lot of beer back then, the water was filthy).

The Old Truman Brewery has a history of brewing dating back to 1666 when Joseph Truman joined the Brick Lane Brewhouse owned by William Bucknall.

The Truman family grew the business and in 1724 opened the Black Eagle Brewery, which became the largest brewery in London and the second largest in Britain.

In 1888 Truman, Hanbury, Buxton and Co. became a public company and gradually moved its production from Brick Lane to a facility in Buxton, where the water was much more suited to the brewing process.

The Truman Brewery, Brick Lane, finally closed in 1988 but the site lives on. Regeneration projects developed during the nineties have turned the area into a vibrant little visitor attraction.

45% of London's visitors are tourists who've travelled to the capital to explore the sights and sounds of one of the world's most celebrated cities.

London's most popular paid for sight is the EDF Energy London Eye and the sights from the top, in one of its capsules, extend for 25 miles. On a clear day you can even see Windsor Castle.

The London Eye greets 10,000 visitors a day, that's around 3.75 million visitors a year, making it the most popular paid for attraction in Britain!

There are 32 capsules carrying a total of 800 people in one rotation. The eye rotates 7,668 times a year and each revolution lasts about 30 minutes.

The London Eye, which at 135 metres is London's fifth tallest structure, was created by architects David Marks and Julia Barfield. It took a total of 7 years to build and is constructed from 1,700 tonnes of British steel.

The wheel is made of 80 spokes and weighs 3,100 tonnes. When it arrived in London it was shipped along the Thames, section by section, and took a week to lift into position.

One of London's earliest visitor attractions was the Great Exhibition, which ran from the 1st May to the 18th October 1851 and was organised by Henry Cole and Prince Albert.

The Great Exhibition was the first in a series of worldwide fairs celebrating the designs and technologies of the modern industrial age. Over 14,000 exhibitors were housed in the original Crystal Palace.

The original Crystal Palace was built by Joseph Paxton in Hyde Park. At 564 metres long by 36 metres high the cast iron and plate glass structure was built especially for the exhibition.

After the exhibition, a new and even larger Crystal Palace was built at Penge Common, near Sydenham Hill. The park opened to the public in 1856 where the palace stood until 1936, when it was entirely destroyed by fire.

Today, Crystal Palace is famous for being a world-class athletics stadium and the park is home to a large collection of life-size dinosaurs. Dinosaur Court, as the collection is known, was commissioned in 1852. When they were unveiled in 1854, they were the first dinosaur sculptures in the world, now they are a Grade I listed building!

London is home to 40,000 listed buildings, 50 theatres, over 200 museums and 100 more notable attractions. On top of that the capital's annual festival calendar holds some 200 events and if you've time for a bit of reading, the capital's got 900 bookshops and 365 libraries with over 17 million books to choose from!

London's largest and most famous library, The British Library was created in 1973. It's home to 250 years worth of collections and houses over 150 million items representing every age of the written word, with some documents being over 3,000 years old.

Most famously the library houses the Magna Carta, one of Leonardo da Vinci's notebooks and the first-ever edition of *The Times* newspaper, from 1788. Within its vaults lie 310,000 manuscripts ranging from Jane Austen to James Joyce, Handel to the Beatles, then there are some 60 million patents, over 4 million maps and a copy of every single British newspaper.

Today, the British Library receives and registers a copy of every single publication produced in the UK and Ireland, that's about 3 million items every 12 months (all that storage requires 625 kilometres of shelving, which expands by 12 kilometres every year – better book a little space for this little book).

The British Museum, Great Russell Street, is the most visited free attraction in Great Britain.

The British Museum owes much of its history to Sir Hans Sloane, a physician, naturalist and collector who, throughout his lifetime collected over 71,000 different objects, which he wanted to be preserved after his death.

When Sloane died in 1753, he gave his entire collection to King George II in return for a £20,000 payment to his heirs. The gift was accepted on the 7th June that year and an Act of Parliament was passed establishing the museum.

The British Museum opened at Montagu House in Bloomsbury on the 15th January 1759. It was the first public museum in the world, free to "all studious and curious persons" and it has been ever since.

Sir Hans Sloane's original collection consisted of a large library, antiquities, coins and medals and natural history specimens. Today the museum is home to over 8 million objects, which span the entire history of the world's cultures: from the stone tools of early man to 20th-century prints.

The Museum of London, London Wall, is home to Europe's largest archaeological archive, which includes 17,000 skeletons.

The museum houses over six million archaeological "finds" – including a Roman bikini believed to have been worn by a female athlete. If you want to find out more about the history of London from prehistoric times to present day, this is the place to go.

London's Natural History Museum, Cromwell Road, Kensington, opened on Easter Monday in 1881. Today it's home to the largest and most important natural history collection in the world.

Inspired by the natural specimens collected by Sir Hans Sloane originally displayed at the British Museum, a larger museum was required to exhibit the additional collections that botanist Joseph Banks had brought back from his voyage aboard Captain James Cook's *Endeavour*.

Sir Richard Owen, superintendent of the British Museum's natural history collection convinced the government that a new museum was required. The Waterhouse Building, which houses the Natural History Museum today, was designed by Alfred Waterhouse.

London's Natural History Museum is home to more than 70 million specimens; 55 million animals, including 28 million insects, 9 million fossils, 6 million plant specimens, more than 500,000 rocks and minerals and 3,200 meteorites.

The National Maritime Museum, Greenwich, exhibits over 500 years of Britain's history at sea. The museum and Royal Observatory are part of the Greenwich Maritime World Heritage Site.

It opened in 1937 and with over two million items, it is believed to be the largest collection of its kind in the world. The museum's library houses over 100,000 historical volumes making it the largest maritime library on the planet.

A landing place for the Romans and once a British naval base, Greenwich has had a long-standing relationship with the sea and its navigation for centuries.

The most notable moment in Greenwich's nautical history was the establishment of the Royal Observatory, which began in 1675 and played a significant role in the history of astronomy and maritime navigation.

The Royal Observatory, Greenwich Park, is home to the prime meridian of the world - 0° 0' 0".

That's an imaginary line that runs from the North Pole to the South Pole, which is known as zero longitude, the point from which all other lines of longitude are measured.

The International Date Line is another imaginary line which runs north to south but 180° away from Greenwich, so the opposite side of the world. Along this line, the world moves into a different day!

conference held in 1884, when world delegates agreed there should be a single universal day. Up until this point, towns all over the world kept their own local time but there was not an agreed international clock (of course the French wanted it in Paris).

It was voted that the "mean solar day" would begin at midnight in Greenwich, London and count on a 24-hour clock. As a result of the decision, the world's 25 different time zones were established from both the East and West of Greenwich.

So, just as the equator divides the northern and southern hemispheres of the world, the zero longitude line divides the East and West. This means that every place on earth is measured in terms of its distance to the east or west of the prime meridian of the world, Greenwich!

London's Science Museum, Exhibition Road, South Kensington, was founded in 1857 with the proceeds of and objects from The Great Exhibition of 1851.

Today it's the UK's most popular destination for all things to do with science, technology, engineering, medicine and design. Exhibits include Stephenson's Rocket, the first steam locomotive, the first jet engine and examples of the first steam engines.

The London Transport Museum began in a garage in Clapham during the 1920s.

The transport collection began when the London General Omnibus Company decided to preserve one of London's first motorbuses and two of its Victorian horse-drawn buses for future generations. It moved to Covent Garden's Flower Market in 1980.

Between 2005 and 2007 London's Transport Museum had a major makeover; today it celebrates over 200 years of London's transport system.

The Imperial War Museum was founded on the 5th March 1917 after the War Cabinet approved a proposal from Sir Alfred Monde MP to create a record of everyone's experiences during the First World War.

The first museum, opened by King George V on the 9th June 1920, was housed inside the Crystal Palace, Bromley. It moved to its current home on Lambeth Road in 1936.

The collection of records set out to commemorate all those, from all sectors of society, whose lives were lost during the war.

Some of the buildings, which now house the Imperial War Museum, formed the central part of The Bethlem Royal Hospital, the world's first psychiatric hospital and where the word "Bedlam" originated.

Today the Imperial War Museum is the world's leading authority on conflict and its impacts. Its collections, which include over 10 million items, are taken from all aspects of war and every individual's experience of it. Records start with the First World War and continue right up to the present day, focusing on Britain, its former British Empire and the Commonwealth.

With over five million visitors a year, London's Tate Modern is the world's most popular art gallery.

The Tate Modern was created in the year 2000 at Bankside, a disused power station converted specifically to house the national collection of international modern art.

The building's 35-metre high, 152-metre long Turbine Hall became the gallery's dramatic entrance area and exhibition space and the boiler house became the galleries.

Since opening, more than 40 million people have visited the Tate Modern making it one of the UK's top three tourist attractions, which generates an associated £100 million every year towards London's local economy.

When the Tate Britain, Millbank, first opened in 1897 it was The National Gallery of British Art. The gallery was officially entitled the Tate in 1932, after the surname of its founder and benefactor Sir Henry Tate.

Sir Henry Tate was an industrialist who made his fortune as a sugar refiner having successfully managed to patent the process of cutting sugar into **dice-sized cubes** (isn't it sweet how people get rich).

The original gallery was specifically designed to house British art from the 19th century. In 1917, the gallery became responsible for the national collection of modern art, and the new galleries, which were funded by Lord Duvan, opened in 1926.

In 1987, with support from the Clore Foundation, the Clore Gallery opened which was able to house the Turner Bequest, which included 300 oil paintings and 30,000 sketches from the great British romantic artist J.M.W. Turner.

By the end of the 1980s, the Tate Millbank could no longer house its collection so a new gallery was needed to display the international part of the collection (hence the Tate Modern) allowing the gallery at Millbank to focus on being the national gallery for British art.

The Victoria and Albert Museum, or V&A as it's known today, is home to the world's largest collection of decorative arts and design.

The museum, founded in 1851, was named after Prince Albert and Queen Victoria. Its collection includes 4.5 million objects, housed across 12.5 acres in 145 galleries, spanning 5,000 years of art.

The National Gallery, Trafalgar Square, houses the national collection of western European painting from the 13th to the 19th centuries.

The gallery began in 1824 when the House of Commons paid banker John Julius Angerstein, £57,000 for his picture collection. The collection was to become the core of a new educational exhibition that was originally displayed in Angerstein's house, 100 Pall Mall.

The National Gallery opened in 1838. It was funded by parliament to be a gallery for all. The centrality of Trafalgar Square made it the perfect location for such a project, which would enable people from all levels of society the opportunity to enjoy its collections.

Today, the National Gallery is free to the public and open 361 days a year. After the completion of the Sainsbury Wing in 1991, the gallery had a total floor space of 46,396 metres, that's about 6 football pitches dedicated to exhibiting the work of some of the finest artists in the world.

The National Portrait Gallery was established in 1856 and owes much of its existence to three biographers and historians – Philip Henry Stanhope, 5th Earl of Stanhope, Thomas Babington Macaulay and Thomas Carlyle.

The gallery was set up to be about people and history rather than art. Its founders believed that the work exhibited should be about the sitter, rather than the quality or character of the artwork itself. It was decided by the trustees that "no portrait of any person still living, or deceased less than 10 years shall be admitted by purchase, donation, or bequest, except only in the case of the reigning Sovereign, and of his or her Consort".

While the rule changed slightly in 1969, the National Portrait Gallery still uses those same guidelines today, when considering what portraits should be added to the collection.

If you're looking for living and breathing exhibits, look no further than London Zoo, the oldest scientific zoo in the world.

The London Zoological Society was founded in 1826 by Stamford Raffles.

The 36-acre zoo was created to house various collections of tropical animals, brought back to London by the society for scientific study. Today it's home to 700 species and 16,000 different animals.

London Zoo is based at Regent's Park, which is also home to the Regent's Park Open Air Theatre, which opened in 1933 with a performance of Twelfth Night. Today it runs a 16-week-long summer season attracting some 140,000 theatre-goers (and if you do go, wrap up warm and don't forget your brolly).

Regent's Park is one of eight Royal Parks, which include Bushy Park, Green Park, Greenwich Park, Hyde Park, Kensington Gardens, Richmond Park and St James's Park.

London's Royal Parkland covers a total of 5,000 acres and offers all kinds of different outdoor activities and respite from busy parts of the city.

During the 1500s, London's Hyde Park was the royal hunting ground of King Henry VIII. Today its 350 acres of greenery are set within some of the most expensive real estate in the world.

Divided into two parts by the Serpentine, Hyde Park is London's largest park making it the perfect venue for some of the capital's largest outdoor rock concerts.

Famous performers have included the Rolling Stones and Queen and in 2005 the park hosted Live 8. During the 2012 Olympics Hyde Park will be home to the triathlon and open water swimming events.

The 260 acres of Kensington Gardens, the setting for Kensington Palace, were originally part of Hyde Park. Today, the gardens are home to the much-loved bronze statue of Peter Pan and the Princess Diana Memorial Playground, which opened on the 30th June 2000 in memory of the late Princess who lived next door at Kensington Palace.

When the news of Princess Diana's death broke on the 31st August 2007, the world's cameras descended upon Kensington Palace. Within hours the gates had become just one of the many fields of flowers that lined parts of Hyde Park or were laid outside St James's Palace and Buckingham Palace.

The number of floral tributes to Diana was estimated to have totalled over one million bouquets. The extraordinary number of flowers perfumed parts of London with the smell of petals.

Over three million people are believed to have lined the funeral route in an effort to pay their last respects to Princess Diana. Over one million gathered to watch the event on giant TV screens erected within Hyde Park.

St James's Park is the oldest (and many think the loveliest) **park in London, it was one of the first parks to be opened to the public and, with over 5.5 million visitors a year, it is one of the most visited parks in Europe.**

The park is uniquely surrounded by three of London's royal palaces; St James's Palace, Buckingham Palace, the Palace of Westminster, now the Houses of Parliament.

The Houses of Parliament, otherwise known as the Palace of Westminster, are situated on the site of the original palace built by Edward the Confessor during the 11th century.

The celebration of Guy Fawkes or Bonfire Night on the 5th of November is a 400-year-old British tradition, which began with the famous Gunpowder Plot to bomb the riverside buildings and kill the reigning king (which would have been the 9/11 of its day).

After the death of Queen Elizabeth I in 1603, previously persecuted English Catholics hoped their religion would be granted more tolerance under the reign of a new monarch. King James I was far from tolerant which incited 13 catholic conspirators to hatch a plan to blow up parliament and in doing so kill the King.

As the plot thickened, 36 barrels of gunpowder were moved into a cellar just beneath the House of Lords. But some of the plotters were getting nervous; concerned that the explosion would harm, if not kill, lots of innocent people.

Eventually, one of the group wrote an anonymous letter warning his friend Lord Monteagle to stay away from parliament on the 5th of November. News of the plot got back to the King and plans were made to capture the conspirators.

Guy Fawkes was caught in the cellar just before he could light the gunpowder! He was then tortured (rather than torched) then executed.

The night he was captured, bonfires were lit throughout London to signify and celebrate the safety of the king.

Today, we celebrate the execution of Guy Fawkes on the 5th of November. All kinds of bonfires and fireworks displays take place throughout the nation.

The Gunpowder Plot hit a nerve in the British monarchy (luckily that was all), so much so that the reigning monarch only visits parliament once a year, on what's known as the State Opening of Parliament. Even today before the opening the Yeomen of the Guard still search the cellars in keeping with a custom that's four centuries old.

The Palace of Westminster buildings are home to the House of Lords, the House of Commons, Westminster Hall, its oldest building, and the Westminster clock tower with its famous bell – Big Ben.

London's Big Ben is nicknamed after the giant bell, which chimes the time in the belfry of the Palace of Westminster's clock tower. The Great Westminster Clock started ticking on the 31st May 1859 and Big Ben first chimed on the 11th of July.

Big Ben was cast on the 10th April, 1858 at the Whitechapel Bell Foundry, East London. The foundry is listed in the Guinness Book of Records as Britain's oldest manufacturing company, which has been in continuous business since 1570.

The bell, measuring 2.28 metres tall and 2.75 metres wide, weighs 13.5 tonnes and is made from tin and copper. After casting, it took two weeks to cool. The mould still hangs on the wall at the foundry.

The numbers on Westminster's clock face measure 0.6 metres tall, the hour hand is 2.7 metres long and the minute hand is 4.2 metres (must have taken a long time to make them!).

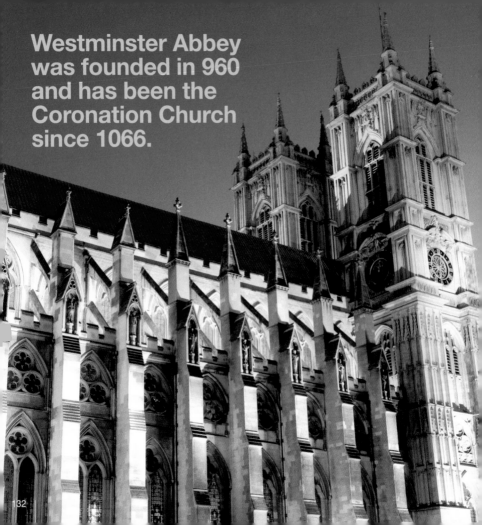

Westminster Abbey was founded in 960 and has been the Coronation Church since 1066.

In its lifetime the Abbey has witnessed 38 coronations, the first being that of William the Conqueror in 1066 and the most recent being the coronation of Queen Elizabeth II on 2nd June 1953.

The Abbey has been the burial ground for 17 British monarchs and commemorates the lives of important people throughout British history including Jane Austen, Lewis Carroll, William Caxton, Oliver Cromwell, Charles Darwin, Sir Isaac Newton and William Shakespeare. In recent history, the royal funerals of the Queen Mother and Princess Diana were both held at the Abbey but their burials have taken place elsewhere.

Westminster Abbey's most recent Royal Wedding was on the 29th April 2011 with the marriage of Prince William to Miss Catherine Middleton. 1,900 people were invited to the church service, which was televised and watched worldwide by an audience of over two billion people.

It's estimated that over 1,000 miles of bunting were sold to mark the wedding, which was celebrated across Britain in over 5,000 street parties.

London would not be London were it not for the royal family. The Crown Estate looks after large parts of the city, with many of its parks, properties and palaces open to the public, drawing millions of visitors to the capital each year.

The Royal Collection is one of the largest most important art collections in the world. Running to over a million objects, it includes most of the contents of 13 royal residences including Buckingham Palace, the Tower of London, Kensington Palace, Hampton Court and the Royal Pavilion Brighton.

Her Majesty's Royal Palace and Fortress, otherwise known as the Tower of London, is famously home to the Crown Jewels of the United Kingdom.

The Tower of London was founded during 1066. The White Tower was built by William the Conqueror in 1087 and used as a prison from as early as 1100.

In over 950 years of history, the Tower of London has been a royal residence, a prison, an armoury, a treasury, a menagerie, the Royal Mint and the since the 14th century the guarded home of the Crown Jewels.

The Tower of London is guarded by Yeoman Warders, otherwise known as Beefeaters, and a flock of dedicated ravens.

In centuries past, the Yeoman Warders had the responsibility to protect the Crown Jewels and look after prisoners. Today, the guards are a tourist attraction in their own right.

The Yeoman Warder Ravenmaster is responsible for the wellbeing of the Tower's raven population. The Tower of London's lucky old ravens are fed raw meat, bought by the Ravenmaster from the Smithfield meat market.

The ravens have been living at the tower since the reign of King Charles II. Legend has it that should the birds ever leave the tower, the monarchy will crumble forever.

When King Charles was told that the birds were interfering with the work of the Royal Observatory, rather than move the birds, he relocated the Observatory, to its site today at Greenwich (he must have been raven mad!).

As well as looking after the ravens, the Crown retains the right to ownership of all unmarked mute swans in open water.

The ceremony of Swan Upping takes place on stretches of the Thames in the counties of Middlesex, Surrey, Buckinghamshire, Berkshire and Oxfordshire.

This tradition dates back to the 12th century, when swans were seen as a tasty dish, today it's an important tradition helping to keep a tally on the health and numbers of newborn cygnets.

The Queen's Swan Uppers take to the Thames in traditional rowing skiffs, wearing a traditional scarlet uniform. The trip takes about five days and when a brood of cygnets is sighted a cry of "All up!" is given.

The cygnets are weighed and measured and examined for any sign of injury. The swans are also given a health check and ringed with individual identification numbers by the Queen's Swan Warden, a Professor of Ornithology at the University of Oxford's Department of Zoology. The swans are then set free.

Buckingham Palace is Her Majesty the Queen's official London residence. It is the largest private house in London and very much regarded as the centrepiece of the British monarchy.

In 1837, Queen Victoria was the first monarch to take up residence in Buckingham Palace. Today the palace is home to the Queen and her husband, the Duke of Edinburgh and used for administrative duties and state entertainment.

As well as being open to the public since 1993, the palace welcomes over 50,000 guests attending various state banquets, events and garden parties each year making it one of the busiest private residences in London.

The oldest and most famous event at Buckingham Palace is the Changing of the Guard, which takes place most days at 11.30 (but check). When the Queen is at home there are four sentries in residence, when she is away there are just two.

The Changing of the Guard is actually called Guard Mounting, the process whereby a New Guard exchanges duties with the Old Guard. The handover, which takes about 45 minutes is accompanied by music from the Guard's band.

Born on the 21st April 1926, Her Majesty Queen Elizabeth II became the British Queen on the death of her father King George VI on the 6th February 1952.

Her Majesty's coronation took place on the 2nd June 1953. Today, the Queen is the second longest serving monarch after Queen Victoria who reigned for 63 years.

The Queen's birthday celebrations take place on the 1st, 2nd or 3rd weekend in June every year. The date is decided by the government and marked by the "Trooping of the Colour" an enormous military parade and march-past where thousands of Soldiers salute the Queen.

It's the biggest royal event of the year and is the day when the Queen's birthday honours are announced.

Queen Elizabeth II is Head of State for 16 commonwealth countries including the British Isles, Australia, Canada and New Zealand and Head of the Commonwealth.

Her Majesty is also Head of the Church of England able to appoint archbishops and bishops and is Head of the Armed Forces – the only person in Britain who, after consultations with her government, can declare when the country is at war and when a war is over.

On top of an extraordinarily busy engagements schedule, which includes attending international events and fulfilling extensive public duties and charitable commitments back home, every Tuesday, Her Majesty the Queens has met with the **British Prime Minister** (that's 60-years worth of PMs!).

During her reign the Queen has sent letters to over 580,000 British and Commonwealth couples to congratulate them on their 60th wedding anniversary and over 175,000 telegrams to those who've reached the ripe old age of 100.

In June 2012 Her Majesty celebrated her Diamond Jubilee, that's the 60th anniversary of her reign as the British monarch. Queen Victoria was the last, and to date the only other British monarch to have also celebrated a Diamond Jubilee.

The Queen was 85 on Accession Day, the oldest monarch to celebrate a Diamond Jubilee. Queen Victoria was 77 when she celebrated hers.

As part of the 1977 Silver Jubilee, marking the 25th anniversary of her accession to the throne, Her Majesty visited 36 different countries and travelled a total of 56,000 miles. The climax of the celebrations took place on the 6th of June when Her Majesty lit a bonfire beacon at Windsor Castle, which started a chain that ran the length and breadth of Britain.

That weekend an estimated 10 million Britons broke out their bunting and rallied around for trestle tables in order to hold enormous street parties up and down the country, over 4,000 took place in London.

At 76, Her Majesty was the oldest monarch to celebrate a Golden Jubilee. The 2002 celebrations included a "Prom at the Palace", where 12,000 members of the public enjoyed a classical concert at the Palace and the "Party at the Palace" where Her Majesty enjoyed performances from Paul McCartney, Bryan Adams, Dame Shirley Bassey, Eric Clapton, The Corrs, Joe Cocker, Phil Collins, Ladysmith Black Mambazo, Annie Lennox and Ricky Martin. The event opened unforgettably with Brian May playing "God Save the Queen" from the roof of the Palace!

To mark 60 years of the Queen's reign the Diamond Jubilee will take place in 2012. The celebrations will centre on an extended weekend on 2nd, 3rd, 4th and 5th June. A brand new bank note and commemorative medal will be issued and celebratory involving millions of people will take place all over Great Britain.

Every spring, the Royal Botanical Gardens at Kew are ablaze with colour as five million spring bulbs come into bloom.

The Royal Botanical Gardens, which became a UNESCO World Heritage Site in 2003, are home to the world's largest collection of living plants!

The 300-acre site is home to 30,000 different living specimens and its herbarium, one of the largest in the world, houses over 7 million preserved plants.

At 4,880 square metres, Kew's Temperate House is not only the largest plant house in the world but the world's largest surviving glass structure, twice the size of Kew's Palm House.

Kew's Palm House, an iconic feature of Kew Gardens, was built between 1844 and 1848. It was designed specifically to house exotic palms, collected by the Victorian plant hunters.

Today rather than hunting for plants, Kew is working to save them. As part of its involvement with the Millennium Seed Bank Partnership, Kew is working with 120 partners across 54 different countries to save the seeds of 25% of the world's most endangered plant species.

While not a traditional garden, Covent Garden was home to one of the world's most famous fruit, vegetable and flower markets. Today, Covent Garden is known for its street entertainers, craft stalls and for home to the Royal Opera House and The Royal Ballet.

Covent Garden's first produce market was started by the Earl of Bedford during the 1500s. By the 19th century it was England's largest fruit, vegetable and flower market.

In 1830, permanent buildings were developed to replace the stalls, which would have stood in the square and by 1871 The Flower Market building, now the London Transport Museum, was the centre of London's flower market.

A century later and Covent Garden's fresh produce traders moved to new warehouses in Nine Elms. The New Covent Garden Market, with over 200 different businesses and 2,500 employees, is the biggest market in Britain.

Today, Covent Garden is visited by 30 million people each year making it one of London's most popular entertainment areas.

The world's first Punch and Judy show, as recorded in Samuel Pepys' diaries, was performed in Covent Garden in 1662.

The Royal Opera House Covent Garden is home to The Royal Opera and The Royal Ballet.

The present theatre, which was built in 1858, is the third theatre on its site. It has four tiers of boxes and balconies and can seat up to 2,256 people.

The first ballet was performed at the venue in 1734 and in 1735 the Royal Opera House ran the first season of Handel's operas, much of his work was premiered at Covent Garden and written specifically for it.

Today, The Royal Ballet is Britain's most prestigious ballet company and The Royal Opera continues to attract the world's finest artists.

The Royal Albert Hall, Kensington, was originally designed as the Central Hall of Arts and Sciences. The name was changed by Queen Victoria to commemorate her late husband and opened in 1871.

The Central Hall of Arts and Sciences was inspired after the success of the Great Exhibition when Prince Albert, the Prince Consort, thought it would be a great idea to have a more permanent public space to hold similar events and exhibitions.

Prince Albert died in 1861 so he never saw the project come to fruition but 6 million bricks and 80,000 blocks of terracotta later the building opened and has affectionately been nicknamed the nation's Village Hall.

Originally designed to hold over 30,000 people, today it has capacity for 5,500. In its lifetime the Royal Albert Hall has held over 150,000 events and hosts over 350 concerts each year, its most famous being the Summer Proms Season, which have been held since 1941.

Prince Albert died in 1861 from typhoid. His death was very sudden and Queen Victoria decided very quickly that a memorial should be built in his honour. She invited architects to put forward designs for a monument, which would be sited just opposite the Albert Hall in Kensington Gardens. Funds for the monument came from public subscription. The winning designer was George Gilbert Scott and the 53-metre high memorial opened in 1872 and the statue of Prince Albert was sited in 1875.

During the 1990s the monument underwent a multi-million pound restoration project. All of the original gold leaf had turned black with air pollution and was replaced with 675 x 20 page books of 24-carat gold leaf. What was initially estimated to be an £11 million job, one of the most complex restoration projects in the world, was completed in 1998 and came in ahead of schedule and £3 million under budget.

In 2011, London's "theatreland" was visited by 14 million theatre-goers. That year there was a record box office taking of over £500 million.

THEATRE

It's no surprise that two of Britain's richest men, Sir Andrew Lloyd Webber and Sir Cameron Mackintosh, have made their fortune while making world-class musicals, most of which have premiered in London's West End.

London's West End is home to over 40 playhouses giving over 16,000 performances each year.

The West End's oldest theatre, The Theatre Royal, Drury Lane, has been entertaining ticket holders since 1663. Today, the theatre belongs to Andrew Lloyd Webber's Really Useful Group, London's largest theatre group, which runs 6 West End theatres, responsible for filling over 11,000 seats each night!

London's oldest-running play, Agatha Christie's *Mousetrap*, is the longest running play in the world.

2012 will mark the production's 60th birthday. For the last 38 years the play has been performed in St Martin's Theatre, West Street. In its 60-year run the cast has included 403 actors, David Raven made it into the Guinness Book of Records as the "Most Durable Actor" after completing a staggering 4,575 performances as Major Metcalfe.

London's longest running musical is _Les Miserables_, which is in its 27th year. In its 26th year, London's 2nd longest musical is _The Phantom of the Opera_.

Having sold over £3.5 billion worth of tickets worldwide, _The Phantom of the Opera_ is believed to be the world's most financially successful live entertainment project to date.

While the West End is home to most of the capital's theatres, London's first playhouse, The Theatre, was built in 1576 by James Burbage in Shoreditch.

William Shakespeare joined Burbage's troupe in the 1580s and the company flourished for the next two decades. After Burbage died, his two sons decided to lease a plot near the Rose, a rival playhouse in Southwark. They demolished The Theatre, carried the timbers over the river and offered Shakespeare a part share in the new building.

Construction for the Globe Theatre began in 1597. It opened in 1599 and for over 14 years it presented many of Shakespeare's greatest plays.

Then in 1613, during a performance of _Henry VIII_, 17th-century theatre pyrotechnics (wadding from a cannon) set the Globe's thatched roof on fire, within hours the entire building had been reduced to cinders (if you can forgive the pantomime pun).

The second Globe, which was rebuilt with a new tiled roof, remained open until all theatres were closed under Puritan administration in 1642. In 1644, in order to make way for housing, the Globe was demolished ending a 45-year period of theatre in the making.

Today's Globe was reconstructed, just 230 metres from where the original theatre began. The project, led by American actor Sam Wanamaker, took 23 years to fund. Finally in 1996, just three years after Wanamaker died, the construction was complete.

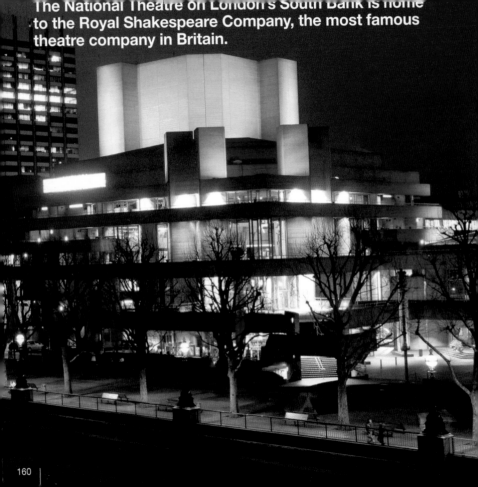

The National Theatre on London's South Bank is home to the Royal Shakespeare Company, the most famous theatre company in Britain.

160

After the formation of the then "New Shakespeare Company" in Stratford in 1879, British actors expressed a long-felt need for a playhouse in London, which could host serious plays rather than productions that were simply economic drivers.

The government agreed a site next to the Royal Festival Hall and the National Theatre was founded between 1963 and 1976 and the Royal Shakespeare Company moved from the Old Vic, into their new home on the banks of the Thames.

In its lifetime the National Theatre has been artistically directed by some of Britain's finest actors and creative talents. The National's first artistic director was Oscar-winning actor Lord Olivier, followed by Sir Peter Hall, Sir Richard Eyre, Sir Trevor Nunn and its current artistic director, Sir Nicholas Hytner.

London's Southbank emerged as a cultural centre as part of the 1951 Festival of Britain. The event, organised by the British Government after the Second World War, had the aim of giving Britons a sense of recovery after the war. While the event took place at venues all over the country, in London, the festival's centrepiece was the Royal Festival Hall.

Today London's Southbank Centre consists of the Royal Festival Hall, the Haywood Gallery, Queen Elizabeth Hall, the Purcell Room and the Saison Poetry Library making it one of the largest art centres in the world.

The Barbican Centre is funded and operated by the City of London Corporation. It's Europe's largest multi-arts and conference venue and home of the London Symphony Orchestra (LSO) and the BBC Symphony Orchestra.

The idea of the Barbican Centre emerged during the 1950s. The area had been severely bombed during the war and in 1951 just 58 people lived in the ward. Construction began in 1971 and in 1982 the centre opened.

Today the arts centre consists of the 1,949-seat Barbican Hall, the 1,166-seat Barbican Theatre, the Pit theatre, a 286-seat cinema and the Barbican Art Gallery.

The LSO was formed in 1904 and moved into the Barbican when it opened in 1982. When it began, the LSO was the first self-governing organisation of its kind in Britain and the first British orchestra to play overseas.

The LSO was famously booked for a concert in New York and due to sail on the Titanic, a last minute change to the booking saved the musicians' lives (bet they would have gone down well too!).

London's Royal Philharmonic Orchestra (RPO) is based at Cadogan Hall, just off Sloane Square. The RPO, dubbed the Nation's favourite orchestra was founded in 1946 by Sir Thomas Beecham.

Every year concert halls across London give over 32,000 performances - that's 621 a week.

The O2 Arena is London's largest, purpose-built concert venue since the construction of the Royal Albert Hall, which opened in 1871.

London's O2 Arena started life as the Millennium Dome, which was built to celebrate the beginning of the third millennium and thus only opened from 1st January to 31st December 2000.

When the new O2 Arena opened in 2007, Anschutz, the development company put on a free event for all the building's employees. Staff got their own private performances from Tom Jones, the Kaiser Chiefs and Basement Jaxx. Next up, the Arena hosted Snow Patrol, who put on a private show for local residents, sponsors and competition winners.

The first public performance took place on 24th June 2007, when Bon Jovi rocked up (and quite literally). In its first 7 months of opening, the O2 Arena sold over 1.2 million tickets. By 2008 it had sold two million making it the busiest venue in the world.

London's most famous stadium is (or was) the old Wembley Stadium, which was situated in the borough of Brent. It was built in 1923, at a cost of £750,000, in exactly 300 days by Sir Robert McAlpine.

It was called the "Empire Stadium" as it was part of the British Empire Exhibition of 1924–25 and was instantly recognisable by its "twin towers" which stood until the stadium's demolition.

The towers were the last part of the stadium to be demolished in 2003. The top of one of the twin towers was erected as a memorial in the park on the north side of Overton Close in the nearby Saint Raphael's Estate.

The "old" Wembley was also famed for its 39 steps that led from the side of the pitch to the Royal Box, where victorious teams would be presented with the trophy and the losers would collect their losers' medals.

The initial stadium hosted a variety of events, but was famed for football. It hosts the annual FA Cup final, England international matches and it was also the place where England won their one and only World Cup in 1966. Wembley has also hosted five European Cup finals as well as the 1996 European Championship final, won by Germany.

Brazilian football legend Pele once said: "Wembley is the cathedral of football. It is the capital of football and it is the heart of football."

It also became a music venue in 1972 and played host to concerts by some of the industry's biggest names such as Queen, Madonna, Tina Turner, Oasis, Pink Floyd, The Who, the Rolling Stones and Elton John. Michael Jackson's 15 appearances were the most by any artist and in the process, he sold over 1 million tickets.

The first event at Wembley was the 1923 FA Cup final between Bolton Wanderers and West Ham United. It became known as the White Horse final (and in those days it was a legal requirement to wear a flat cap to a football match - just kidding!).

The match was played only four days after the stadium's completion and vast numbers of supporters and casual observers turned up for the occasion, far exceeding its 127,000 capacity. In a bid to control the crowd, the police used a white horse by the name of Billy to push the crowds back to pitch-side in order for the game to be played.

When it got underway, Bolton went on to win 2-0 with David Jack having the honour of scoring the first-ever goal at the stadium. It is estimated 140,000–200,000 filed through the 104 turnstiles that day with a further 60,000 spectators locked outside. Every FA Cup final from thereafter was ticketed!

The last FA Cup final to be played at the old Wembley was in 2000 and in front of 82,000 when Chelsea beat Aston Villa 1-0. The last-ever match was between England and Germany later that year, which the Germans won 1-0.

The new Wembley Stadium opened in 2007. It was built by an Australian firm called Multiplex at the staggering cost of £798 million, although the total cost of the project (including local transport infrastructure redevelopment and the cost of financing) was estimated to be £1 billion.

It is the second largest stadium in Europe with a capacity of 90,000. It was delivered late after a string of delays and Multiplex made a substantial loss on the project.

Wembley is instantly recognisable by the 134-metre (440ft) high arch. With a span of 317 metres, it is the longest single-span roof structure in the world and, uniquely for a stadium, requires beacons for low flying aircraft.

Today's Lord's is the third of three cricket grounds established by Thomas Lord between 1787 and 1814. The current Lord's houses the world's oldest sporting museum.

If Wembley is the home of football, then Lord's is the home of cricket. The earliest recorded game was between Marylebone Cricket Club and Hertfordshire played at the current venue in St John's Wood in 1814. Middlesex County Cricket Club plays its home matches at Lord's.

Lord's is one of two Test match cricket grounds in London with the other being south of the River Thames. The Kia Oval, home of Surrey County Cricket Club, is situated in Kennington and traditionally hosts the last Test match of the summer.

The first recorded match at the Oval was in 1868 against an Australian Aboriginal touring side. 20,000 spectators gathered to watch the game. The first-ever Test match was played at the Oval between England and Australia in 1880.

In 1882, Australia won the Test series *The Sporting Times* mocked England's efforts claiming that English cricket had died, and "the body will be cremated and the ashes taken to Australia".

The English media dubbed the next tour of Australia (1882-83) as the quest to regain the Ashes. A small terracotta urn was presented to England by a group of Melbourne women on the tour with its contents said to be the ashes of an old bail.

To this day, the two countries compete for an urn in the Test match series, named "The Ashes", although the original urn has never been presented or displayed as a trophy (indeed, the Ashes have never left Lord's, no matter who has won them - much to the irritation of the Aussies!).

The London marathon is one of the world's top five marathons and has been run in the capital since 1981. It is run over 26 miles and 385 yards and has raised over £450 million for charities since its inception.

The London marathon holds a place in the Guinness Book of Records for being the largest fundraising event in the world when, in 2009, £47.2 million was raised by its participants.

The first London marathon was held on 29 March 1981, more than 20,000 applied to run. 6,747 were accepted and 6,255 crossed the finish line on Constitution Hill. By 2009, 746,635 people had completed the marathon and in 2010, a record 36,549 people took part.

Wimbledon is home to the All England Lawn Tennis and Croquet Club. Every year, the Wimbledon Championships are played on its lush ryegrass courts, one of the four major grand slam events in world tennis.

Dating back to 1877 it's the oldest championships and regarded as the most prestigious by competitors. It's the only major to be played on grass too. There are five main events (men's singles, women's singles, men's and women's doubles and mixed doubles.)

The Wimbledon Championships of 1877 were the first-ever organised tennis championships in the world. Today, the two-week long grand slam event attracts some 480,000 spectators and uses a total of 15,000 balls a tournament... (well, actually the nice library said 1250 dozen – which should be kept at 20°C).

If you read our *Little Book of Balls* you'll discover that a top class 'tennie' must bounce 53 – 58 inches when dropped from 100 inches onto concrete!

As well as the tennis, Wimbledon is home to the largest single sporting annual catering operation carried out in Europe. Its 1,800 staff serve up (well it's a different kind of service I guess):

300,000 cups of tea and coffee

250,000 bottles of water

200,000 glasses of Pimm's

190,000 sandwiches

150,000 bath buns, scones and doughnuts

135,000 ice creams

100,000 pints of draught beer and lager

32,000 portions of fish and chips

7,000 litres of dairy cream

25,000 bottles of champagne

12,000 kg of smoked salmon and ...

... 28,000 kg (112,000 punnets) of English strawberries.

The home of rugby union is also based in London with the national stadium located at Twickenham and named after the district. It is the largest rugby stadium in the world with a capacity of 82,000. It is the second largest stadium in the United Kingdom and fifth largest in Europe.

As well as hosting England rugby internationals, it has been the venue for a number of rock concerts as well. Iron Maiden, REM, Bon Jovi, Genesis, U2, The Police, The Eagles and The Rolling Stones have all played at Twickenham.

Before the land was bought by the RFU in 1907 for just £5,500, it was used to grow cabbages, thus Twickenham's affectionate nickname of the "Cabbage Patch".

Every spring, crowds line the banks of the River Thames for the annual Boat Race between the Universities of Oxford and Cambridge (how do those two always get into the final?).

The first Boat Race was held in 1829 and it has been held annually since 1856 with the exception of the two world wars. Cambridge has the honour of most wins with 80 compared to Oxford's 76 and one race ended in a dead heat.

In 2012, it was estimated that 250,000 watched live from the riverbanks with millions more watching live on television (sadly one jumped in and swam out to bring the race to a halt – talk about putting a dampener on things!).

There are over 20 rowing clubs based along the banks of the Thames with the London Rowing club the oldest after being established in 1856.

London's most famous sporting occasion, the 2012 Olympics and Paralympic Games will take place between the 27th July and 12th August and 29th August and 9th September respectively (let's just hope the sun comes out).

Us Brits are obsessed with the weather so it's a good job they've timed the Olympics for the warmest month of the year.

July in London is the month that tends to see the lowest rainfall and the highest temperatures – an average of 22-23°C. The summer evenings throughout June, July and August can be deliciously long with it not getting dark until after 9pm.

London's warmest day took place in August 2003 when the capital's temperature reached 35.3°C – the highest temperature ever recorded in the city. In Greenwich, the highest ever temperature hit 38.1°C.

That day it was so hot that the heat caused train tracks to buckle, overhead cables to sag, even the London Eye overheated with the temperature in the capsules reaching over 30°C.

Because of the heat generated by such a densely urbanised area, wintertime in London tends to feel a few degrees warmer than the rest of Britain. Nevertheless, December is still the wettest and coldest month for London and it's not like the capital hasn't experienced some extreme climatic conditions throughout its populated history.

In October 1091, London was hit by Britain's first-ever recorded tornado. The T8 tornado, which would today be equal to an F4, destroyed London Bridge, demolished the church of St Mary-Le-Bow, flattened 600 houses and claimed the lives of 2 people.

In December 2006, a tornado swept the streets of Kensal Green, north-west London injuring 6 people and damaging 100 properties causing a repair bill of over £10 million.

In 2010, London experienced its worst winter for over 50 years. Over 10 inches of snow fell in parts of the capital suspending bus and overground train services as well as flights at Gatwick and Heathrow but it wasn't cold enough to freeze the Thames.

During the 1500s extremely long periods of below-zero conditions along the Thames created ice so thick that is was possible to walk on, ride horses on, drive carts on and even hold carnivals on.

London's largest frost fair was held in 1814. As soon as it was safe to stand upon, traders took to the ice to set up stalls selling hot food and drinks, printers began printing souvenirs promoting products that had quite literally been "bought on the Thames" and all manner of entertainment took place.

The building of the new London Bridge altered the flow of the Thames making the current too fast for the river to freeze over. The 1814 Frost Fair was the last-ever event of its kind.

By the end of the summer 2012, London will have hosted the Olympic events three times. The first London Olympics took place in 1908 and then again in 1948.

During July and August 2012, 300 different sporting competitions will take place at 34 venues throughout London and the sailing events will take place in Weymouth, Dorset.

The games will feature 26 sports, 39 disciplines and 302 medals are up for grabs. The 300 different events are expected to attract over 1 million international spectators and will include 10,500 athletes from over 205 different nations.

Over 8.5 million tickets have been made available and a total of 350,000 ticket holders are expected to attend the games each day.

London's £500 million Olympic Stadium, Stratford, which took 3 years to be built, will be able to seat 80,000 people making it the third largest stadium in Britain.

And for any Olympic injuries, London's home to some of the oldest hospitals in the world!

Having endured the Black Death, the Great Fire of London and the Blitz, Guy's and St Thomas' Hospital is one of the most well-known hospitals in the world. The hospital began in 1170 when the monks at Southwark infirmary named their hospital after the martyr Thomas Beckett. When the hospital opened it had just 40 beds.

Guy's Hospital is named after Thomas Guy, a wealthy landowner who leased the land to build the new hospital, which opened in 1725. On his death, Guy gave his entire fortune to the hospital which was so enormous that it enabled the institution to run on its own for two centuries until the birth of the NHS in 1948.

The Royal Marsden was the first hospital in the world dedicated to the study and treatment of cancer. The hospital was founded in 1851 by Dr William Marsden and originally called the Free Cancer Hospital.

St Bartholomew's Hospital still stands on the site it was built on in 1123. Locally known as Barts, the hospital is the oldest hospital in London and the UK.

London has long been called "a world in one city".

A 2005 survey examining the diversity of London's religious and ethnic population claimed that on top of 300 different languages, the capital was home to 50 non-indigenous communities, each with a population of over 10,000 people.

A 2007 survey suggested that 31% of London's residents were from an ethnic minority with 42.3% of city dwellers belonging to groups that are non-white British (how wonderfully colourful).

Today, London is one of the most ethnically diverse cities in the world and has been for more than 2,000 years. Since ancient times London has been the heart of Great Britain's international trade and commerce. The constant influx of traders and travellers making their way up the Thames has made London an exotic, wealthy and welcoming city for foreigners.

Centuries later, as the British Empire expanded, London's multi-national links and colonial history has made it home, and often safe haven, to people and communities from many different countries.

And, as people from all over the world have settled in the city, so have their cultures, cuisines, customs and religions (and that's what makes London such a special place on earth today).

"London is a roost for every bird" Benjamin Disraeli.

25% of Greater Londoners come from outside of Great Britain. The capital's community represents over 270 different nationalities.

According to the Office for National Statistics, while the lion's share of the capital's population claim Christianity as their religion, Greater London is home to 40% of Britain's Muslim population, 50% of Britain's Hindu population, 60% of Britain's Jewish population, 30% of Britain's total Sikh population and 24% of Britain's Polish community.

The first Muslims to settle in London arrived during the 19th century. They were sailors from Somalia and the Yemen. Today, London's Muslim community come from all over the world making up 600,000 of the metropolitan population.

London's first mosque, the Fazl Mosque, opened in October 1926 in Southfields, near Putney. It was the first-ever Ahmadiyya mosque built in Great Britain.

The Baitul Futuh Mosque in the southwest suburb of Morden (at the end of the Northern Line), in the borough of Merton, is believed to be the largest mosque in western Europe.

The London Central Mosque, also known as the Islamic Cultural Centre, was completed in 1978 in Regent's Park. Famous for its incredible golden dome, the main worshipping hall can hold up to 5,000 people. The mosque is joined to the Islamic Cultural Centre, which was officially opened in 1944 by King George VI.

In 2007, over 500,000 Indian people were living in the capital making London home to more than 1/2 of Britain's Hindus.

In the Brent and Harrow boroughs, the Hindu religion is celebrated by some 20% of the population.

Brent is home to the Shri Swaminarayan Mandir, London's first Hindu temple. Built in Neasden, it was the first-ever traditional Hindu temple to be built in Europe.

Affectionately known as the Neasden Temple, it was carved out of 2,820 tonnes of Bulgarian limestone and 2,000 tonnes of Italian marble. The stone blocks were exported to India, then shaped individually by some 1,500 local craftsmen and then shipped back to London for the final assembly.

The first stone was laid in June 1993 and some 26,300 pieces later this giant 3D jigsaw became the world's largest traditionally built Hindu Mandir in the planet!

Although Polish people have been travelling to the capital as traders and diplomats since the 1500s, Polish communities began to settle in London after the First and Second World Wars.

In 1940, the entire Polish government including the president and prime minister and 20,000 soldiers were moved to the capital. After the war, Polish Prisoners of War as well as large numbers of political emigrants found refuge in London and during the 1950s as Britain eased immigration laws, the capital became home to more and more Poles.

For centuries the Polish migrants and their descendants have contributed enormously to life in London and in Britain as a whole.

Michael Marks, founder of Marks and Spencer emigrated from Poland to Britain in 1882 and Kent-born Sir Jack Cohen, founder of Tesco, is of Polish descent, so are Ed and David Miliband.

Today, it's estimated over 123,000 Poles live in London, with the largest community living in the Hammersmith area.

London's Jewish community has been part of the capital's history for over 1,000 years.

Jewry Street, inside the financial district of the City of London, is named after the first Jewish community who settled within the city gates during the 1200s. It was also the area they returned to some 350 years later, after Oliver Cromwell allowed Jews to return to Britain. Today, London's Jewish community is one of the longest standing populations of London.

During the 17th century large numbers of Jewish migrants found refuge from Russian and German persecution in London's East End, living and working in the Spitalfields and Whitechapel parts of London.

By the turn of the 20th century there were over 300,000 Jewish people living in East London with over 150 synagogues. Today, just four remain, Bevis Marks being the oldest.

Built in 1701, Bevis Marks, Whitechapel is the oldest synagogue in London. It was built by East London's Spanish and Portuguese Jewish community. Today, it's the only synagogue in Europe to have held continuous worship for over 300 years.

BEIGEL BAKE

BRICK LANE BAKERY

No.159 OPEN 24 HOURS 7 DAYS Tel. 071-729 0616

The East End's Brick Lane, once a major Jewish community, is now the curry capital of London and home to the capital's most famous bagel bakery (try saying that after a few drinks).

Beigel Bake opened in the 1960s and is perhaps all that remains of what was once a thriving Jewish community in the East End of London.

Today, Beigel Bake, 159 Brick Lane, is open 24 hours a day seven days a week. It's most famous for smoked salmon and cream cheese bagels (and the salt beef sandwich, served up on rye, is pretty good too).

Today the area is home to the largest Bangladeshi community outside of Bangladesh. The Brick Lane celebrations of Baishakhi Mela, the Bengali New Year, are the biggest celebration outside of Bangladesh and West Bengal.

Over ¼ of the British Chinese population live in London, that's 100,000 Londoners.

London's Chinatown began in Limehouse docks of the East End. The first Chinese quarter dates back to the 18th century when Chinese sailors working for the East India Trading Company settled in the docklands opening shops and restaurants for other Chinese seamen.

At the end of the Second World War, Limehouse had been destroyed by the Blitz but British soldiers returning from the Far East kick-started a new demand for Chinese cuisine in London's West End.

As Gerrard Street, the site of some of London's first European restaurants and the notorious 43 Club, began to develop a reputation for international cuisine, new opportunities opened up for London's Chinese. By the end of the 1950s Chinatown had been born.

London's present day Chinatown district includes Gerrard St, the bottom half of Wardour St, Rupert St and Rupert Court, a section of Shaftesbury Avenue, Lisle St, Macclesfield Street and Newport Place, Newport Court and Little Newport Street.

Chinatown boasts 78 restaurants, 53 local shops including herbal remedy treatments and reflexology specialists and 12 bars and pubs.

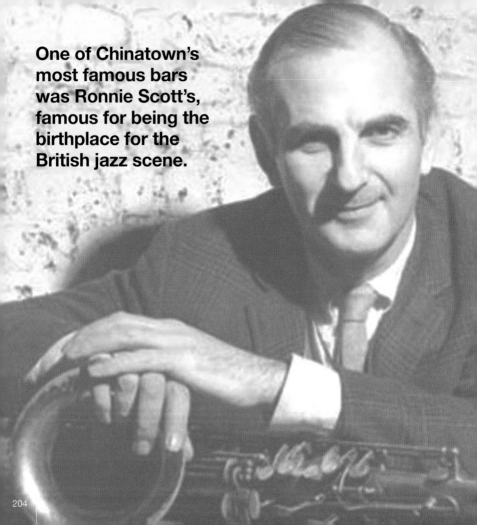

One of Chinatown's most famous bars was Ronnie Scott's, famous for being the birthplace for the British jazz scene.

Ronnie Scott's opened in Chinatown on Friday 30th October 1959. Today it's one of the oldest surviving jazz clubs in the world.

Ronnie Scott's began in a basement premises at 39 Gerrard Street. The dream began 12 years earlier after Scott, a talented tenor saxophonist, blew his savings on a trip to New York to experience the US jazz scene. Post-war Musician's Union restrictions made it impossible for American jazz musicians to come to Britain to perform in person.

Inspired from his two-week tour, Scott returned to England and he and fellow business partner Peter King began looking for a place where they could establish a club. They decided upon 39 Gerrard Street and after a £1000 loan from his stepfather the lease for the basement was signed, Ronnie Scott's was born.

The appearance of jazz giants including Zoot Simms, Jonny Griffin, Stan Getz, Al Cohn and Ben Webster meant a larger premises was soon required. During the summer of 1965, 47 Frith Street was acquired for the new club and it has been there ever since.

Every January, London's Chinatown is adorned with lanterns as celebrations begin for the Chinese New Year.

The Chinese New Year marks the beginning of the lunar calendar and is celebrated between the first new moon and the first full moon in January.

Every year, on the Sunday closest to the beginning of the new lunar calendar, thousands of people flock to Trafalgar Square to enjoy performances, dancing and singing as the festival floats parade from Trafalgar Square to Rupert Street. Celebrations culminate in an epic fireworks display and Chinatown's streets are filled with entertainment and all kinds of food stalls.

London's celebrations of the Chinese New Year festivities are the largest outside of China. Alongside the Notting Hill Carnival, Chinese New Year is fast becoming London's 2nd largest multicultural event.

The Notting Hill Carnival began on the August Bank Holiday of 1959. The first event was held in the local town hall. It was created in an attempt to resolve the racial unrest in the area while celebrating the culture and traditions of West London's Afro-Caribbean population.

61% of Britain's Afro-Caribbean population live in London. The Great British capital is home to over 350,000 British Jamaicans. That's 7% of all Londoners.

Although London's links with the Caribbean date back to the 16th century and Britain's role in the slave trade, today most of the capital's Caribbean community are 2nd or 3rd generation of those who came to London after the Second World War.

When the Empire *Windrush* sailed into London's Tilbury docks in 1948 with 492 passengers from Jamaica and Trinidad, it marked a significant moment in the start of the Caribbean migration to Britain. That moment would become an important part of London's post-war history.

The brave individuals who walked the gangplanks of the Empire *Windrush* in 1948 were the first large group of West Indian migrants to arrive in Britain after the Second World War, thousands would follow.

Post-war Britain experienced severe labour shortages so the British Government encouraged immigration from the West Indies and other countries within the British Empire. In 1948 the British Nationality Act gave all those living within the Commonwealth full British Citizenship.

Most of the *"Windrush"* generation
became a major part of the workforce
who reconstructed London after the war.

EMPIRE WINDRUSH

Most were employed to repair London's transport network or build, what was then, the beginning of the National Health Service.

During the 1950s London's first Afro-Caribbean settlers moved to Brixton and Notting Hill Gate. But times were far from settled for London's new citizens.

Both Brixton and Notting Hill Gate suffered poor housing provision and high levels of economic deprivation. Many incomers were refused housing on the basis of their race, with many boarding houses and restaurants specifically turning Afro-Caribbeans away.

By the end of the 50s, racial tensions in London, and other large UK cities, were beginning to mount. Various pro-white, anti-immigration organisations became increasingly vocal, overtly protesting about the number of migrant workers in Britain. It was a tense time.

Fuelling inter-racial tensions in West London, the infamous Notting Hill landlord Peter Rachman was violently driving out white "sitting tenants", those protected from rental increases, and filling his slum-like residences with West Indian immigrants, who had no choice but to pay the high rents.

As a result of his unethical actions, the term "Rachmanism" entered the Oxford English Dictionary describing "Landlords buying up slums to fill with immigrants at extortionate rents".

Inter-racial tensions exploded in the Notting Hill area of London during the summer of 1958.

The Notting Hill Race Riots began on Friday 29th August after an attack on a Swedish woman who was married to a West Indian.

That night, over 300 of London's "Teddy Boys" took to Bramley Road carrying out a series of racial attacks on a number of Notting Hill's West Indian residents. The violence continued every night until the 5th September, during which time the Metropolitan Police made 140 arrests.

In 1963, the appalling housing conditions in London's Notting Hill led Reverend Bruce Kenrick to set up the Notting Hill Housing Trust. The trust began to tackle corrupt landlords and improve housing within his Notting Hill Parish; today it's one of the largest housing associations in Greater London.

In 1966, the Notting Hill Housing Trust gave birth to Shelter, the largest housing and homeless charity in Britain.

In the last 40 years, changes in housing legislation and drastic improvements to Notting Hill's iconic townhouses have made the area one of the most desirable places to live in London.

211

The Notting Hill Carnival, the largest festival of its kind in Europe, is London's biggest multicultural celebration, created 50 years ago by the Westbourne Grove's West Indian community.

The Notting Hill Carnival began in 1959 in St Pancras Town Hall. The event was organised by Claudia Jones as a response to recent racial attacks and as a way of tackling diminishing race relations in the area. Despite being held indoors, the event was a huge success and in 1966, with the help of the London Free School (a big bunch of hippies really), the first outdoor carnival took to the streets.

What began in 1966 as a small street festival celebrating the traditions of the capital's Afro-Caribbean culture is today one of the largest carnivals in Europe. Some 40,000 volunteers step up to make it happen and over 1 million party-goers attend the event which takes place every August bank holiday.

In the past, the party has attracted up to two million festival goers so, after Rio, London's Notting Hill Carnival is the 2nd largest street festival in the world!

London's diverse population makes the city home to 300 different languages.

The capital's very own language, cockney rhyming slang, is believed to have originated from London's East End.

The exact origins of London's cockney rhyming slang are unclear. It's not really its own language because the words used are English and it's not really a dialect because those who can speak rhyming slang can also speak English.

Many believe cockney rhyming slang originated in London's East End during the 17th century, a secret language spoken amongst the costermongers, the East End's street traders, to hide criminal activities from the recently established police force, London's Peelers. Others believe it came from London's prisons as a way for inmates to communicate without alerting eavesdropping guards.

Where and whenever it originated, cockney rhyming slang is surprisingly prolific in the English language. Sayings like "I haven't heard a dicky bird", "use your loaf", "stop rabbiting on", "I'm on my tod", "he half-inched it" and "telling porkies" come from the cockney rhyming slang vernacular.

Popular cockney words and phrases include:

Dicky bird = word
Loaf of bread = head
Rabbit and pork = talk
Tod sloan = alone
Half-inch = pinch
Porkie pies = lies
Apples and pears = stairs
Rosy lea = tea
Barnet fair = hair
Butcher's hook = look
China plate = mate
Currant bun = sun
Deep sea diver = £5
Dog and bone = phone
Hampstead Heath = teeth
Hank Marvin = starving
Ruby Murray = curry
Mince pies = eyes
Pen and ink = stink

Since the 1980s, London's cockney code has seen a significant resurgence. The old rhyming style has been adopted and adapted by the nation's adolescents. To create new meanings and the modern day tongue the new cockney slang is known for using the names of famous celebrities.

Ayrton Senna = a tenner/£10
Britney Spears = beers
Claire Rayners = trainers
Damon Hill = the pill
David Gower = shower
Jack Dee = pee
Tony Blair = flares or hair

The word cockney, often used to describe the working class of London's East End, originates from the 14th-century term "cockeneyes" which described a misshapen, or a cock's, egg!

Since the 1600s, the word cockney was used to describe any Londoner born within earshot of the Bow Bells of London's Cheapside.

The Bow Bells or the bells of St Mary-Le-Bow Church, Cheapside, are some of the most famous church bells in the world. Their chimes are said to have called Dick Whittington back to London so that he could become one of the city's most famous Lord Mayors.

"I do not know says the Great Bell of Bow" was the fitting ending to the medieval nursery rhyme *Oranges and Lemons* and the BBC World Service recorded the Bow bells to broadcast during the Second World War as a symbol of hope to the free people of Europe.

While St Mary-Le-Bow was destroyed during the Great Fire of London in 1666, the church was rebuilt by Sir Christopher Wren. On 11th May 1941, the church was destroyed once again by German bombers and the 12 Bow Bells were re-installed in 1956 and first rang on the 21st December 1961. Today, St Mary-Le-Bow is the the leading peal ringing bell tower in the City of London.

London's cockney traders were originally known as costermongers, fruit and vegetable sellers who traded from market barrows in the markets of Cheapside and the East End.

As well as their own language, costermongers had their own uniform and even their own alternative royal family.

The Pearly Kings and Queens of London's Cockney East End date back to 1875.

The East End Costers were a caring bunch, known for running a "whip round" to raise money for those in need. When orphan Henry Croft, a street sweeper and rat catcher, fell into their care, he was inspired by their generosity and caring attitude.

Looking for a way to also raise funds for the needy, Henry Croft decided to decorate an entire suit in the coster's pearly style and "The Original Pearly King" as he has been described, was born.

Henry Croft died in 1930, over 400 "Pearlies" attended his funeral and his legacy continued, by 1975, there was a Pearly King and Queen for every London borough. Today, the pearly tradition is 125 years old and London's Pearlies continue Henry's commitment to raising funds for a number of charities throughout each of the Greater London boroughs.

Because of its incredible views over the City of London and Westminster, the top floor of City Hall has been dubbed "London's Living Room".

Measuring 45-metres high, City Hall was designed by Sir Norman Foster. It was built between 1999 and 2000 and has 10 above-ground floors, which accommodate 600 GLA staff and the Mayor of London.

The rounded shape of City Hall means it has 25% less surface area than the traditional rectangular city buildings. This makes it more energy efficient.

Instead of using the mains supply, City Hall's water is drawn from two boreholes beneath London's water table. The water is used to cool the building and then to flush the loos.

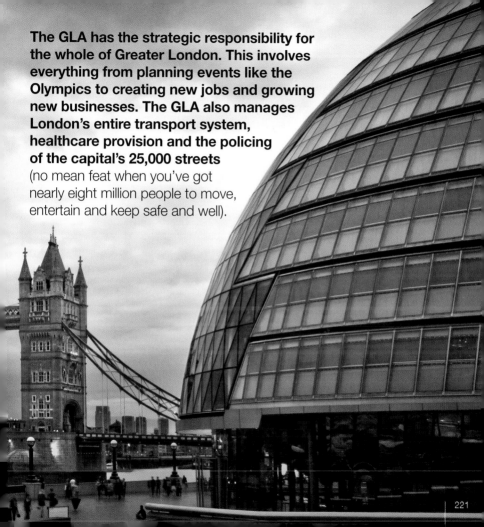

The GLA has the strategic responsibility for the whole of Greater London. This involves everything from planning events like the Olympics to creating new jobs and growing new businesses. The GLA also manages London's entire transport system, healthcare provision and the policing of the capital's 25,000 streets (no mean feat when you've got nearly eight million people to move, entertain and keep safe and well).

Keeping London moving is the job of Transport for London.

Transport for London (TfL) was set up in 2000 and is responsible for all of London's streets and main road routes, the bus, underground and overground rail networks, London's walking and cycle routes and the licensing of all taxis and private hire transport services (eek).

TfL employs some 20,000 staff which provide Londoners with 2 billion bus journeys a year, 1 billion underground journeys and 800 million journeys on the rail networks.

Of the 27 million passenger journeys made in London every day, 80% are made on London's road network and TfL manages all 580 kilometres of them.

In 2010, London authorities filled a total of 159,000 potholes across the capital at a cost of £11.2 million.

On any given day over 5,000 holes are dug into London's roads as part of major maintenance works as the GLA tries to keep on top of the wear and tear.

Delays caused by roadworks cost the London economy around £750 million. In fact, 20% of the UK's total traffic congestion happens in London, which is said to cost the British economy a total of £2 billion a year.

Whether congested or flowing freely, vehicles don't get far in London without a stop at one of the capitals 6,000 traffic lights.

London has a long-standing relationship with traffic lights. It was the first city on earth to have one (stop it!).

On 10th December 1868, the first-ever traffic signal was erected outside the Houses of Parliament. Similar to semaphore signals used on the railways, the gas-operated lamp had a green arm and a red arm, which indicated the flow of traffic (but how did drivers know what the colours meant?).

The gas lantern, which, enabled the signal to be used at night was hand operated and turned at its base so the light faced the oncoming traffic. On 2nd January 1869, the traffic signal exploded, seriously injuring the policeman operating it.

Today, London's 6,000 traffic signals are powered by electricity!

London was the first city in Britain to employ parking wardens (stick that on your window).

The first 40 traffic enforcement officers took to London's streets in search of illicit motoring activities on 19th September 1960. They were part of the Metropolitan Police Force.

London's first-ever parking ticket was issued to a Dr Thomas Creighton who was nicked while attending a heart attack victim in one of London's West End hotels!

50 years on and the capital's parking enforcement officers are slapping an average of 1,300 parking tickets on windscreens every day.

In London in 2010 a total of 8,700 vehicles were clamped, over 47,000 were impounded and London's 33 authorities issued a total of 4,151,901 parking tickets (that's about £337 million).

With or without a parking ticket, London is the most expensive place to park on the planet!

Research carried out by Colliers International in 2011 put London's parking charges 20% higher than anywhere else in the world.

P Pay at meter

Display ticket
Max. stay   2 hours

Monthly charges to park in the City are about £670, in the West End it's £630. In Zurich, Hong Kong, Rome and Tokyo the same would cost about £430. At £335 a month, New York is even cheaper.

In 2009, London's road users clocked up a total of 30.5 billion miles travelling across the capital making London the most congested place to drive in Great Britain.

In 2010, a report by TomTom suggested that Britain's roads were some of the most congested in the world with 35% of London's roads regularly experiencing traffic jams (not sure you need to buy a sat nav to work that one out).

Reducing the congestion, and the pollution it causes, on London's roads has been a major objective for the Mayor of London's office and the Greater London Authority.

We forget that little more than a century ago, driving, let alone owning a car was a rare luxury.

In 1920, just 100,000 driving licences were registered to London addresses but by 1930 this figure had risen to 261,000. And, as the number of drivers on London's roads increased, so did the number of road accidents with an average of three Londoners dying each day as a result of road traffic.

The boom in car ownership in London began after the Second World War. By the mid 1960s 1.5 million cars were registered in London.

Today 2.5 million cars are registered in London, not to mention vans, trucks, public buses and London's iconic hackney carriage.

The Austin FX4, probably the most famous-looking of all London taxis, first graced the streets of London in 1958. The design held its own for 50 years.

The first public carriages to clatter the capital were second-hand, horse-drawn coaches that had once belonged to the aristocracy.

As a way of recouping the enormous costs of running a horse and carriage, London's wealthy leased their coaches to the less well-off gentry who hired them to get around town.

As the coaches aged they were replaced and the old ones sold to innkeepers and merchants who started London's first unofficial taxi trade, which needless to say was dangerous and they charged excessively.

In 1624, Captain John Bailey organised London's first official taxi rank, which opened on The Strand with four coaches and coachmen. London's first cabbies had a uniform and were told by Captain Bailey exactly what to charge.

The term "hackney" comes from the French word "hacquenee" which described the breed of horse particularly good at pulling London's first carriages.

The word "cab" comes from the French word "cabriolet", which was a speedy little French-designed carriage, introduced to London in 1823.

From the 1830s onwards, two types of public carriages were available in London; the sexy little French number, which whipped about the city open topped and all and the much slower second-hand "growler", which was more suited to collecting large numbers of people and their luggage from London's growing number of stations.

London's first motorised cabs were electric and arrived in the city in 1897 (if only we'd kept it that way). They were called Bersey's after Walter C. Bersey, the manager of the London Electrical Cab Company, but eventually nicknamed "hummingbirds" because of the noise they made. By 1898 over 50 hummingbirds flew about town but were withdrawn in 1900 for being unreliable.

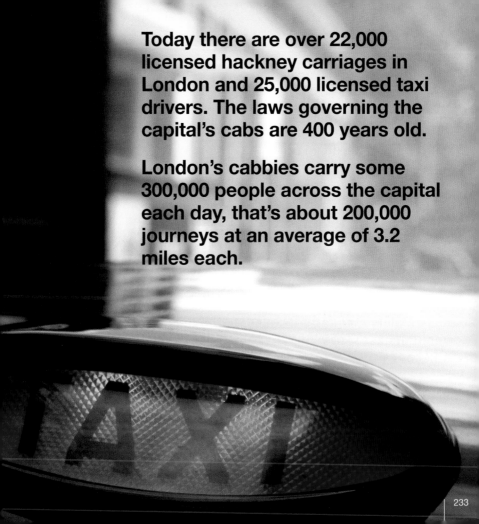

Today there are over 22,000 licensed hackney carriages in London and 25,000 licensed taxi drivers. The laws governing the capital's cabs are 400 years old.

London's cabbies carry some 300,000 people across the capital each day, that's about 200,000 journeys at an average of 3.2 miles each.

Since 1865, all London taxi drivers have to take a test called The Knowledge.

The Knowledge test takes between two and four years to pass. It's based on learning 320 routes, known as runs, which include knowing thousands of London's streets and landmarks, each within 6 miles of Charing Cross (so if you ever see someone bombing around on a moped staring at a clipboard on the front, that's what they're doing).

For all modern-day maps, the centre of London is recorded as Charing Cross and has been for over 700 years.

When the wife of King Edward I, Queen Eleanor died in 1290 in Lincoln, the grief-stricken monarch decided to erect 12 memorial crosses along the route as her coffin made its way back to London.

Today, the statue of Charles I, near Trafalgar Square, marks the site where the original Charing Cross would have stood. From that spot, officially speaking, Manchester is 184 miles away, Liverpool is 198, Rome some 1,118 miles out and the sun a good 93,000,000!

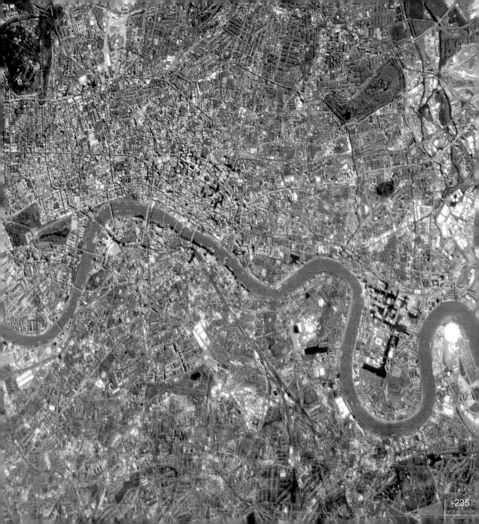

Trafalgar Square is the most famous square in Great Britain.

Its name commemorates Britain's greatest naval victory, the Battle of Trafalgar in 1805. The site is owned by Her Majesty in Right of the Crown and managed by the Greater London Authority.

Before it was cleared and re-designed during the 1800s, Trafalgar Square was originally home to the Great Mews; the courtyard and stabling for Whitehall Palace.

In 1812, one of London's great architects, John Nash redeveloped the area with a new street running from Charing Cross to Portland Place and a large open cultural space which would be open to the public. The open area was given the name of Trafalgar Square in 1830 and has been at heart, if not the heart of London ever since.

Trafalgar Square has had a significant role in British democratic history. For over 150 years it's been the centre of all manner of demonstrations, protests and important political rallies.

This tradition is still very much supported by the Mayor of London today. If organisations want to hold a public meeting or demonstration in the square there's a set of guidelines and an online booking form (it's a PDF of course – Public Demonstration Form!).

Rallies in Trafalgar Square can only take place at weekends or bank holidays, you're not allowed to protest after dark, if you want to plug in a PA system, nothing more than 79 decibels please (and you'll find the power supply at the bottom of Nelson's Column!).

Nelson's Column was designed by William Railton to commemorate Admiral Nelson who famously defeated the French at the Battle of Trafalgar.

The stone column, which was carved from Dartmoor granite took three years to build and was erected in 1843. The five-metre statue of Nelson was created by sculptor Edward Hodges Baily and carved out of Craigleith sandstone from Scotland.

When the statue was restored in 2006, the restoration team was unable to find a new supply of stone, the Craigleith Quarry closed over 60 years ago.

Fortunately a source became available during the restoration of Donaldson's School for the Deaf in Edinburgh. The salvaged sandstone was donated to London by Watson Stonecraft and is part of the patched up Nelson, who looks out over London and the square today.

The four bronze panels at the base of Nelson's Column are cast from guns captured during Nelson's battles. The four lions, designed by Sir Edwin Landseer, are cast in bronze, believed to be from melted down French cannons.

The lions, which are 20 feet long and 11 feet tall, are said to protect the monument. Legend has it that if Big Ben ever strikes 13 times, the enormous sculptures would come to life (but we're not sure if that information is something we can re-lion!).

The four fountains became part of Trafalgar Square in 1845.

Although they were designed to add further aesthetics, the fountain's main purpose was to reduce the floor space available to Trafalgar's ever-increasing number of potential rioters and protesters.

The fountains have just had a £200,000 makeover; complete with LED lights and a brand new 24-metre water jet! They normally operate between 8.30am and 11pm but in April 2012, due to a hosepipe ban, the water supply was turned off.

Every Christmas, Trafalgar Square is lit up by a giant Norway fir, a gift to Britain from the Government of Norway for Britain's role during the Second World War (and who isn't in need of a good spruce during the winter?)**.**

Traditionally on the 31st December every year, Trafalgar Square is filled with midnight revellers as people gather to hear the chimes of Big Ben as it rings in the New Year.

These days London's New Year's Eve celebrations culminate around the London Eye as over 7,000 kilos of explosives set the capital's sky alight with one of the world's most breathtaking fireworks displays.

Trafalgar Square was once famous for its 4,000-strong flock of pigeons, which it became illegal to feed in November 2003.

The droppings of Trafalgar's grey feathered friends were costing the GLA £140,000 in damages to Nelson's Column each year (no shit). Today, anyone caught feeding Trafalgar's pigeons is at risk of a £500 fine (or go to jail - do not pass go!).

The London Stone, caged within Cannon Street, is believed to be the oldest waymark in London.

The ancient limestone block is thought to have been the "millarium" for Roman London, marking the spot from which all distances were measured during the Roman occupation.

The earliest written references to the existence of such a milestone date back to the 10th century and it became a formal landmark in 1198 when it was marked on maps as "Lonenstone" or "Londenstane".

The London Stone is sometimes referred to as the Brutus Stone or Stone of Brutus, named after the legendary Trojan founder of London some 3,000 years ago. Other legends state that the stone was part of an ancient stone circle from Ludgate Hill and others believe it was the stone from which King Arthur miraculously removed Excalibur.

Today, the London Stone is situated opposite Cannon Street tube station. The local pub is even named after it (it's just around the block!).

However you find your way to London, you'll certainly find some of the city's routes incredibly congested. In the 1960s London's rush hour was just that, an hour of heavy traffic in the morning and again in the evening (now it lasts all day!).

With 11 million drivers and motorcyclists taking to London's roads each day, congestion is one of the capital's biggest challenges.

Today, motorists account for 22% of the capitals carbon emissions, making London's air quality the poorest in Great Britain.

In centuries gone by, the air pollution in London, largely caused by the burning of fossil fuels was so prolific that it caused toxic fogs known as "pea-soupers".

At its peak, Battersea Power Station, just one of London's large-scale power stations, was burning over 1,000,000 tonnes of coal a year. The burning of coal releases high levels of sulphur dioxide, a major pollutant into the atmosphere.

On the 4th December 1952, windless weather conditions and high levels of air pollution carpeted London in a yellowy grey fog, so thick that it brought the city to a standstill.

The fog, which became known as the Great Smog took a few days to clear and when it did, it left a soot-like toxic film of dust on the tops of London's window ledges and outdoor surfaces.

Although Londoners were used to smoggy conditions, the medical statistics presented the following year showed that the Great Smog had put some 20,000 people on sickness benefit and contributed to over 4,000 deaths.

Research carried out later suggested that over 12,000 people lost their lives and that reducing London's sulphur dioxide levels was crucial to the long-term health of the capital.

The impacts of the Great Smog of 1952 called for much tougher regulations and the updating of the Clean Air Act in both 1956 and 1968.

Today, London's air quality is much, much better but it's still the poorest in Britain. However, more and more efforts are being made to improve air quality and reduce London traffic's toxic emissions.

Cities like London have a massive role to play in the reduction of greenhouse gases. Worldwide, cities consume around 75% of the world's energy while producing about 80% of its emissions.

London is responsible for 8% of the UK's carbon emissions, in 2006 that was about 44 million tonnes of CO_2. By 2025, just because of population growth, that figure's estimated to grow to an annual 51 million tonnes.

Interestingly, because of the high use of public transport and the densely populated living conditions, per capita, Londoners have a lower than average carbon footprint than the rest of the UK.

Nevertheless, the Mayor of London and his team and the GLA have made some brave calls to cut road congestion and carbon emissions, the congestion charge being one of the city's boldest and most contentious moves yet.

The congestion charge was introduced to Central London on the 17th February 2003.

The Congestion Charging project cost over £160 million to install and requires a further £110 million each year to operate. The system is based on a series of cameras, which photograph and then database all the vehicle number plates entering the congestion zone area. The computer system then matches registration numbers with those who have paid the congestion charge and those who haven't (clever).

By law, profits raised from the congestion charge coffers have to be ploughed back into London's public transport network. Fair enough.

The first daily congestion charge was £5 a day, in July 2005 this went up to £8 and today it will cost you £10 to enter Central London (it doubles fast!). Failure to pay the charge by midnight the day after entering the zone carries a hefty fine of £50 if paid within 14 days, £100 if within 28 days and £150 thereafter (ouch).

According to TfL, before the congestion charge was introduced an average of 334,000 vehicles a day travelled through the charging zone. Within the first 5 years of charging an average of 70,000 fewer vehicles a day use the same area.

By its 5th birthday, TfL's statistics claim the capital had seen a 5% shift from private car usage to public transport, walking or cycling and bus travel was up by 45% – to 6.3 million bus journeys a day!

251

Over 90% of the capital's residents live within 400 metres of one of the network's 19,500 bus stops and today over 6.5 million passengers will have caught a bus from one.

London's bus network is one of the most sophisticated in the world (and it's got the largest fleet of wheelchair accessible buses on earth too).

Around 8,000 of London's iconic red buses operate 700 different routes across Greater London. Nearly 50% of all Londoners use the bus at least twice a week.

London's famous double-decker bus, the AEC Routemaster, was introduced to the capital's bus routes in 1956. It's another iconic symbol of London. Its robust design withstood over half a century of service and has inspired all kinds of tourist gifts and paraphernalia.

London's Routemaster was a design classic, 2,700 were manufactured in total and over 1,000 are still running today. In fact, some of the first-ever Routemasters to ride London's streets are still in service. A number still operate on London's two heritage routes (people love 'em).

London's first double-deckers were horse-drawn and called omnibuses (omni is latin for everyone - get it). So, too, were the capital's first open-top buses. Today, London's open-top buses are a great way to take a tour of the capital's top sights.

London's first-ever sightseeing bus tour took place on the 11th June 1951, as thousands flocked to the capital to see the Festival of Britain.

Known as "Service J", the non-stop circular tour was promoted as "around the town for half a crown" (12½p doesn't rhyme so well!) and every visitor who stepped aboard got their own free London Transport Guide Book. The first sightseeing route included Buckingham Palace Road, South Kensington Station and Bloomsbury Place.

Service J ran until 1992 when it was replaced by "The Original London Sightseeing Tour".

Today the company is owned and operated by Arriva and trades as The Original Tour, a great above-ground way to see the sights as you travel around London.

The quickest way to travel around London is on the London Underground...

The London Underground transports one billion people a year, that's 3.5 million passenger journeys a day (no wonder it feels crowded!).

The Underground service has 12 different lines serving over 270 stations. 45% of the network runs underground (funny that) in some of the oldest tunnels in the world.

The world's first-ever Underground rail service opened in London on the 10th January 1863. The line was known as the Metropolitan or "the Met" and ran for six kilometres (that's four miles), between Paddington and Farringdon Street.

To build the Met, streets along the route were completely excavated, tracks laid in the trench and then covered over with a brick-lined tunnel. This became known as the "cut and cover" method, which was quick and effective but, in an already bustling city, caused all kinds of above-ground congestion.

Once the Met had proved a success, other rail companies were keen to get involved and by Christmas 1868 the Metropolitan district had opened a line between Westminster and South Kensington and by 1884 the Circle Line had been completed (100 years later the Circle Line was known as the party line as students....hundreds of them....would buy the cheapest ticket, carry a barrel down and go round and round and round!).

In 1890, with the introduction of the first deep-level electrical railway line the London Underground became affectionately known as "the tube".

By 1900 the Central London Railway opened from Shepherd's Bush to Bank, the first Central Line, known then as the "Two Penny Tube".

By 1906 the Baker Street and Waterloo Railway opened a service from Baker Street to Kennington Road (now Lambeth North) and The Great Northern, Piccadilly and Brompton Railway opened a line between Hammersmith and Finsbury Park, now part of the Piccadilly Line.

By 1907, the Charing Cross, Euston and Hampstead Railway opened a line from Charing Cross to Golders Green and Highgate, now part of the Northern Line.

The last Underground line to be entirely completed was a section of the Jubilee Line, which ran from Stanmore to Stratford and opened in 1999.

Today the London Underground operates on a total of 402 kilometres of track on a network that's 140 years old.

The famous London Underground symbol was first used on the network's stations in 1908.

The symbol's sans-serif typeface (i.e. no fancy twirly bits) was designed by Edward Johnston in 1916 and is still in use today (and thanks to Transport for London for letting us use it on the front cover). It was updated in 1979 and the font, which is owned by TfL, is called New Johnston in the original designer's honour.

1908 also saw the publication of London's first tube map, which combined, for the very first time, five different companies operating eight different lines.

The first diagrammatic map of the London Underground was published in 1933; it was designed by Harry Beck (a work of art).

Beck was an Underground employee at the time and realised that because most tube journeys took place underground, the physical location of each station and the exact distance between them was kind of irrelevant, only the topology really mattered.

Beck created the map in his spare time. His simplified version used straight lines, horizontal, vertical or those at a 45% angle to make it easier to read.

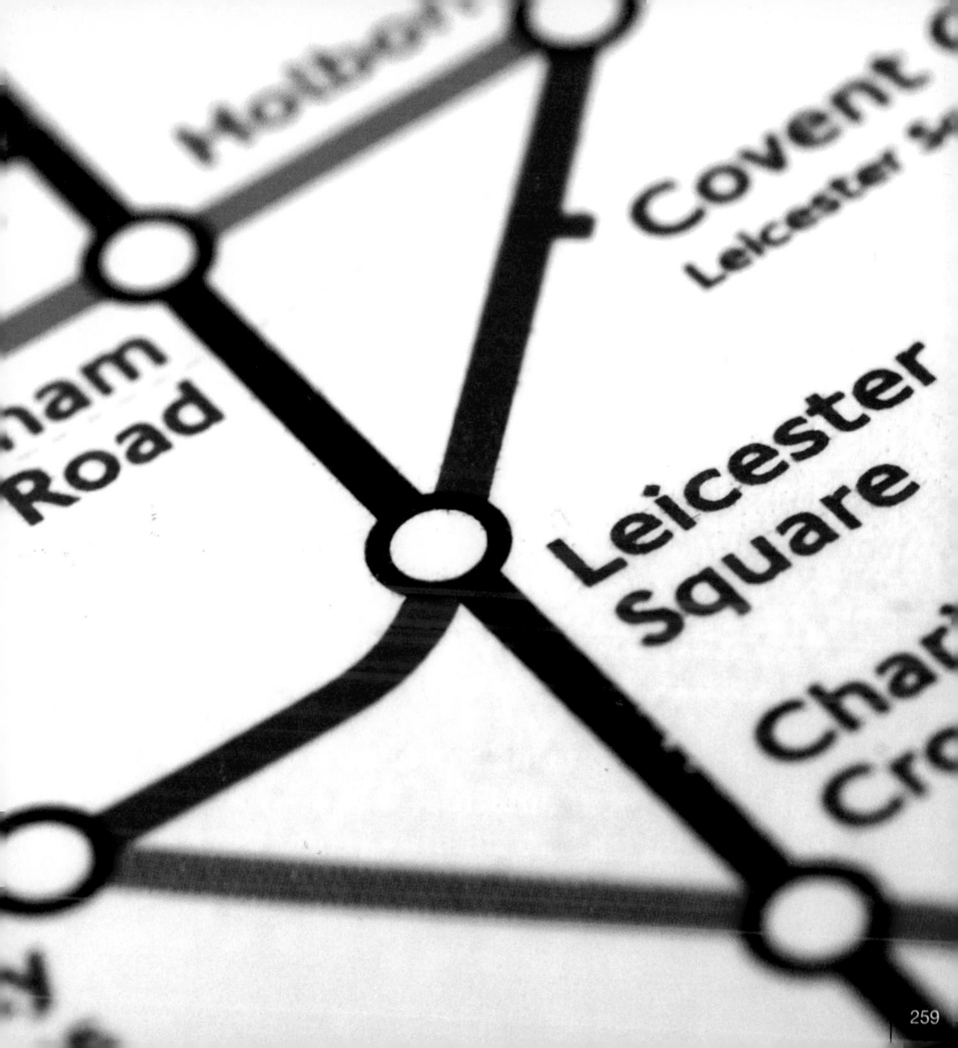
Covent
Road
Leicester
Square

Beck's map was first published as a pamphlet in 1933 and was a huge success. Beck, who lived in Finchley, continued to develop London's tube map until 1960. One of his original maps is preserved on the wall of the southbound platform of Finchley tube station.

The tube's first escalator was installed at Earl's Court in 1911, today there are a total of 426 of them. Waterloo has 23 making it the busiest underground station on the network.

At 60-metres high, the escalator at Angel is the steepest on London's Underground.

The first aluminium carriages were introduced to the District Line in 1952. Today, the London Underground has 4,134 passenger carriages in operation with each train travelling a total of 184,269 kilometres a year.

In 2010, the London Underground's trains ran a total of 69 million kilometres, that's 1,750 laps of the world or 90 trips to the moon and back (that's one giant trundle for man!).

The recordings "Mind the Gap" and "Stand Clear of the Doors Please" were recorded by sound engineer Peter Lodge in 1969. While his original recordings are still in use, if you take the Piccadilly Line you might just hear the familiar tones of Tim Bentinck, otherwise known as David, from The Archers!

The Oyster card was introduced across London's transport network in 2003. It's a travel card, season ticket and a kind of pay as you go card that can be topped up at over 4,000 places across London, over the phone and online.

Since launch, over 34 million Oyster cards have been purchased and over 7 million are in regular use. Today more than 70% of bus and tube passengers use Oyster cards as a way to travel and the numbers of non-fare-paying passengers across all of London's transport networks have dramatically dropped.

With millions of Londoners and a further 1.1 million commuters using the capital's transport network each weekday, keeping the service safe and crime-free is the responsibility of the British Transport Police.

London has three different police forces, The Metropolitan Police, who look after the Greater London area, the City of London Police who deal with crimes within the square mile or City of London borough and the British Transport Police who look after the railways and buses.

In 2010, TfL and the British Transport Police were able to announce that crime on the Underground and Docklands Railway had fallen by 4%.

METROPOLITAN POLICE

In 2010 and with over 12,000 individual CCTV cameras in operation, the police recorded an average of 13 crimes for every million passenger journeys on London's Underground. That same year the service carried 1.1 billion travellers!

London was the first city in the world to have its own official police force.

The origins of the British police force came from the Saxon method of organising people in groups of ten, known as "tythings". Each tything had a tything-man as its representative and every ten tythings had a "hundred-man" who reported to the "shire-reeve" or Sheriff of the county.

After the Norman Conquest, while little remained of the Saxon system, the tything-man's role grew into what became that of the parish constable, a responsible, unarmed but able-bodied citizen who served the parish for one year, reporting to the local Justice of the Peace.

During the 17th century, the parish constables in London were assisted by the "night-watchmen", local men, often old boys who'd fallen on hard times, who were paid to guard and patrol the capital at night.

However, as London's population rapidly expanded, existing methods of governing the capital were becoming more and more futile and it was time to reform London's enforcement of law and order.

"The Bow Street Runners", founded by author and chief magistrate for Westminster at Bow Street Magistrates Court, Henry Fielding were paid for by government funds and were London's first, unofficial police officers.

The Bow Street boys were a cross between a barrister and "thief-taker" (a form of private detective who solved small crimes for a fee). Their job was to serve warrants and court summons, arrest criminals and sometimes solve crimes. They were based at No. 4 Bow Street and worked directly for the court.

After Henry Fielding retired as a magistrate, his brother John continued to develop the service. With the introduction of a patrol on horseback (the Bow Street Riders!), the Bow Street Runners were becoming ever more effective.

Within a few decades, Bow Street had created a successful policing system that formed the basis upon which London's "New Police" would be designed.

The Metropolitan Police Force first took to London's streets on the 29th September 1829. Its founder was Home Secretary Sir Robert Peel; London's first official policemen: "peelers" or "bobbies" were named after him (robbers wouldn't have been right!)**.**

The first Metropolitan Police Force had a budget of £194,126 and was made up of 17 divisions, each with 4 inspectors and 144 constables. Armed with just a truncheon, London's first bobbies wore dark blue long-coats and a tall hat (which they could stand on to look over walls – true!)**.**

The responsibility of organising the Metropolitan Police was given to Colonel Charles Rowan and Richard Mayne. The commissioners were based at No. 4 Whitehall Place, the back courtyard of which was used as a police station and became known as the very first Scotland Yard.

Tucked just behind St James's Park Underground station, New Scotland Yard is most famous for its revolving sign, which rotates over 14,000 times a day!

Today, London's Metropolitan Police Service has a worldwide reputation. The Greater London operation, which polices 1,587 square kilometres and over 7.8 million people, is made up of 140 police stations, 32,500 sworn-in police officers, 14,000 staff, 230 traffic wardens, 4,300 Police Community Support Officers and 3,600 volunteers. Across the Greater London area the force operates 8,000 vehicles, 22 marine vessels, 120 horses and 3 helicopters (there's dogs too but we didn't count them!).

The 2011 Royal Wedding required the services of some 5,000 police officers and the 2012 Olympics will be utilising squads and services from every single department.

London's fire brigade is the largest fire and rescue service in the UK. It's the third largest fire-fighting authority in the world.

London's first firefighters were part of fire insurance brigades, developed after the Great Fire of London, one of the worst disasters London has ever seen.

After a long hot summer, one that brought drought to many parts of the capital, the Great Fire of London began on the 2nd September 1666.

During the 1600s London had a population of 500,000 people and was the largest city in Britain. Accommodation within the old Roman wall of the city was cramped and overcrowded.

While thatched roofs had been banned because of the previous fires in the city, the lion's share of medieval London was built out of timber and covered in pitch, a black waterproof resin similar to tar (hence the saying pitch-black) and quite flammable.

The fire started at around midnight at Thomas Farriner's bakery on Pudding Lane.

As the fire spread it travelled down Fish Hill and when it reached the Thames it ignited warehouses and London Bridge. By Monday the blaze headed north into the heart of the City, by Tuesday it had destroyed St Paul's and had leaped the River Fleet, keenly making its way towards Whitehall and the residence of King Charles II.

Samuel Pepys, famous diarist and Clerk to the Royal Navy observed the beginnings of the inferno from the Tower of London. Having watched how rapidly and easily the fire spread across the tightly packed houses, he suggested to the King that the only way to tackle the conflagration quickly enough was to explode everything in its path.

Fire-fighting orders at the start of the fire had been delayed due to the panic and indecisiveness of London's Lord Mayor, Sir Thomas Bloodworth.

The call to demolish buildings using fire hooks came too late and by the time the King took command, the entire city was alight.

By Wednesday, the strong winds that fanned the fire had died and the Tower of London garrison used controlled gunpowder explosions to level a sufficient number of buildings to create a large enough break to halt the fire.

The Great Fire of London engulfed the entire area of London within the City wall. The inferno destroyed a total of 13,700 homes, 87 churches, The Royal Exchange, The Guildhall and the original St Paul's Cathedral. 70,000 of the city's 80,000 inhabitants were made homeless, becoming refugees in the then fields of Islington and Highgate.

The cost to rebuild London after the Great Fire stood at £10 million (over £1 billion in today's money)**, at a time when London's annual income was just £12,000.**

With the help of Sir Christopher Wren the city took 30 years to rebuild itself. Ironically, much of the new design was taken from the old street plan but the lanes were widened and the city's new buildings were built out of brick and stone – not wood (solid thinking!).

The most significant structure
to be built after the Great Fire of
London is The Monument.

Completed in 1677, at 61 metres high, the giant memorial column, designed by Sir Christopher Wren, stands not far from Pudding Lane, marking the spot where the Great Fire began.

Another much smaller memorial, the Golden Boy of Pye Corner, found between St Paul's Cathedral and Smithfields Market marks the furthest extent of the fire.

In 2008/09 the London Fire Brigade received 229,308 emergency 999 calls. 29,215 of which were fires, 13,841 of which were regarded as serious, making the London Fire Brigade one of the busiest fire-fighting organisations in the world.

274 years after the Great Fire and the streets of London were raised once again, under the attack of the German Luftwaffe.

During the first 22 nights of the Blitz, London's wartime firefighters fought nearly 10,000 fires. By the time peace had been declared, London's fire service had attended over 50,000 calls.

The London Blitz lasted from Saturday 7th September 1940 until the 11th May 1941.

The first attack took place on the Saturday afternoon at 4pm. No less than 320 German bombers escorted by 617 German fighter planes formed a 20-mile wide swarm of aircraft, which filled 800 square miles of the sky along the Kent coast.

At around teatime, over 300 tonnes of explosives fell on the capital, 500 were killed, 1,400 injured. It was the first and last daylight raid on London.

From the 7th of September until the 2nd of November, London was bombed every night, that's 57 nights in a row. Despite health and safety warnings, the London Underground was one of the most popular places to shelter during the Blitz. At the peak of the bombing, some 177,000 took cover overnight in the tube.

On the 10th May, London saw its last bombardment but the Germans hit hard. That night 542 bombers attacked the city dispatching 700 tonnes of explosives. 1,400 civilians were killed, 5,000 homes were destroyed and 12,000 Londoners were made homeless. 2,000 fires were reported and an estimated 700 acres of London were alight, some parts burned for three days.

During the Blitz London saw no less than 73 raids, a total of 20,000 people were killed, 1,400,000 were made homeless and over 3,000 unexploded bombs had to be dealt with.

With 75% of the capital flattened it was little short of a miracle that St Paul's was still standing (or anyone else for that matter!). This photo, one of the most iconic images of London at war was taken by Herbert Mason, from the rooftop of the Daily Mail, Tudor Street.

At 365 metres high and weighing a mere 65,000 tonnes, the dome of St Paul's Cathedral is one of the highest in the world. Between 1710 and 1962, it was the tallest building in London.

St Paul's Cathedral was founded in 604 AD and built in dedication to St Paul the Apostle.

In its time the site of St Paul's has been home to five different cathedrals. The design of the building today was created by Sir Christopher Wren and built between 1675 and 1710. It was the first church to be built after the Reformation (when Henry VIII took the Church of England from the jurisdiction of the Pope into the Crown).

The Church of England Cathedral has held many state occasions for the United Kingdom including the funerals of Lord Nelson, the Duke of Wellington and Winston Churchill and more joyously jubilee celebrations for Queen Victoria and Queen Elizabeth II.

Wren's cathedral, built from Portland Stone, which came all the way from Dorset, was officially completed on the 25th December 1711. During 1716, the total cost of the project came to just over £1 million, £142 million in today's money.

Wren was told by the experts that he needed "more massive pillars" (health and safety again!)**. So he put them in. Recently cleaners discovered that not one of them reached the ceiling!**

Despite being a major target, St Paul's Cathedral survived the Blitz. Its miraculous resilience to the German bombing raids made St Paul's an important symbol during the war years.

During the Second World War, St Paul's Cathedral was struck on four occasions.

The first one was a time delayed device, which, had it detonated, would have destroyed the entire cathedral and left a 100-foot crater. It was successfully defused by the Royal Engineers, under the command of Temporary Lieutenant Robert Davies, who was awarded the George Cross as a result of his action (and we assume made permanent!).

The last bomb to hit St Paul's got lodged in the shell of the dome. Fortunately it fell out before it could set fire to any of the timbers. At the height of the air raid, Sir Winston Churchill telephoned the Guildhall to insist that all fire-fighting capability be sent to St Pauls to protect what had become a national symbol of survival.

"At all costs, St Paul's must be saved." Sir Winston Churchill

Today, St Paul's is London's Cathedral, the cathedral of the Diocese of London and houses (as the word cathedra suggests) the seat of the Bishop of London.

For over 300 years, St Paul's Cathedral has been the religious heart of the City of London. The buildings have survived two world wars and are an iconic part of the history and skyline of the City of London.

The City of London is the oldest part of the capital.

At just 1.12 square miles (2.90 square kilometres) **in area, the City has been affectionately nicknamed the "Square Mile".**

Though perhaps little in size, London's Square Mile has an enormous history, which dates back some 2,000 years when the Romans first crossed the Thames and civilised the first-ever British capital, Londinium.

By the start of the 2nd century, Londinium had outgrown the Roman capital of Colchester and was soon to become the largest Roman settlement in Britain.

During the Roman occupation, the Square Mile would have been surrounded by a moat and 18-foot wall. The old city, whose old walls still form the boundaries of the City of London today, was founded in 47AD as Londinium.

London Wall was the first Roman defensive structure to surround Londinium. It was built during the late 2nd century and its construction and adaptation continued up until the 4th century, when the Romans left the country.

London Wall was one of the largest Roman structures ever built in Great Britain.

Its construction was so substantial that even after the Great Fire of London and the Blitz, the highest surviving remnants of the city were always that of the old Roman wall.

Today, London Wall is one of the main roads that runs through the City. Remains of the wall can be found along the Barbican Estate, at the Museum of London and just outside Tower Hill tube station.

The gates that were cut into London Wall are still very much a part of the fabric of the City today.

Aldersgate, Ludgate, Aldgate, Moorgate and Bishopsgate are named after the gates that would have once marked entrances into the ancient city.

Aldgate, the city's oldest and most easterly gate, was one of the four original gates within London Wall.

Built by the Saxons, the name Aldgate comes from the Saxon word "aelgate" meaning "open to all". During the 1300s, Geoffrey Chaucer lodged in one of Aldgate's upstairs rooms.

During 1415, Moorgate was cut out of London Wall to provide access to the open moorland lying to the north of London.

The Moorfields would have been one of London's first public parklands. Today, Finsbury Square and Finsbury Circus are located in what would have been the original moor.

There's even a Cripplegate, a curious name which some believe came from the numbers of beggars outside the city wall (well – slightly handicapped-gate wouldn't have had the same tone). Others think that Cripplegate may have come from the Anglo-Saxon word "crepel", which meant covered passageway

During Roman times Ludgate would have marked the entrance to what was once Londinium's burial ground (now Fleet Street!).

The City of London is represented by the banner of arms of the Corporation of the City of London.

The flag is made up of the St George's Cross and in the top left canton, an upturned sword, which is believed to represent the one that beheaded St Paul during the 6th century.

While the City's Coat of Arms has never been officially granted, you'll see it on numerous buildings throughout the city. It bears the motto "DOMINE DIRIGE NOS" meaning "Lord, direct us".

The dragons that stand as supporters on either side of the shield are another iconic emblem of the City of London.

The City of London is run by the City of London Corporation; the oldest local authority in England (and we don't just mean its members!).

The City of London Corporation manages and provides all the local services required by the professional and financial institutions of the City as well as the City's local community.

So, as well as looking after 11,000 residents and the 320,000 workers who work in the City each weekday, the City of London Corporation runs the quarantine station at Heathrow, the Port Health Authority for the whole of the Thames tidal estuary and three of the UK's premier wholesale food markets.

CITY OF LONDON

On top of that, the City of London operates its very own police force and runs England's central criminal court, the Old Bailey.

It also looks after five of London's bridges, including the Millennium Bridge and Tower Bridge and further afield it funds the maintenance of 10,000 acres of green space including Hampstead Heath and Epping Forest (ah, peace at last).

Dating back to medieval times, the City of London Corporation is led by the City's Lord Mayor and the Court of Aldermen (similar to the House of Lords) and the Court of the Common Council (similar the House of Commons).

One of London's most famous Lord Mayors was Lord Richard Whittington, the inspiration for the famous pantomime Dick Whittington.

Contrary to the fairytale, the real life Dick Whittington was far from poor. Born during the 1350s, Richard Whittington made his fortune as one of London's mercers, a cloth trader who dealt mainly in silk, wool and velvet.

In his lifetime Richard Whittington was four times the Lord Mayor of London and three times Master of the Mercers' Company.

His fortune, all of which is in trust to the Mercers' Company today, enabled Whittington to become a moneylender to the king and finance all kinds of philanthropic projects in London.

These included public toilets, a public library, a hospital and Whittington College; 56 almshouses in Felbridge, East Grinstead, which are still sheltered homes.

Today for the one-year term he or she has in office, the Lord Mayor of the City (not to be confused with Boris Johnson the Mayor of London) lives at London's Mansion House.

Built in 1758 and just opposite the Bank of England, the Mansion House is a rare example of a Georgian town palace.

After the Great Fire of London, the palatial residence was specifically designed for the city's Lord Mayor enabling he or she to entertain and hold office in style (it's hardly changed and well worth a visit).

The City of London borough is divided into 25 wards, each ward elects an Alderman and between 2 and 10 commoners, who represent them in the court. Both courts are held every four weeks at the Guildhall (the City's town hall).

The City's court is often referred to as the "Grandmother of Parliaments". Westminster's Houses of Parliament are based on the very same model.

Votes for the Lord Mayor's post are held every Michaelmas (that's the 29th of September to you and me) but only the Freemen of London's Livery Companies have the right to cast a vote.

Every Midsummer's Day, London's Freemen vote for the next Sheriff of London. In times gone by the Sheriff had a very busy job, responsible for collecting taxes and the law and order of the City. Today, the Sheriff is primarily concerned with matters of justice and the administration of the Old Bailey, England's central criminal court.

The Old Bailey is England's Central Criminal Court where the major criminal cases of England, Wales and London are heard. The building today dates back to 1907 but the court's records date back as far as 1674, when it was rebuilt after the Great Fire.

The Old Bailey is built on the site once occupied by Newgate Prison, a notorious medieval Jail. Today the courts overlook the area where many executions took place. The last beheading took place in 1820 and the last public hanging in 1868.

For centuries, executions were a major public event, thousands have gathered outside Newgate to watch people hang or be beheaded. Some onlookers even rented rooms in local houses so they didn't miss the event (medieval "axe factor" I guess.).

As well as Newgate, Tyburn, at the far end of Oxford St next to Hyde Park, was home to another of London's famous execution spots. The Tyburn site was named after the River Tyburn.

The first executions at Tyburn, which would have overlooked Hyde Park, began in 1196. It's estimated that up until 1783 over 50,000 men and women were hanged on that spot.

The first hangings took place from the branches of a number of local trees. The Tyburn Tree, a triangular wooden construction, was developed to hang up to 24 people at a time (no point hanging around!).

Hundreds of thousands of people would attend the Tyburn hangings, which became a bit of a public festival. So much so that in 1783 all hangings were moved to Newgate Prison.

Today, if you wander over to the traffic island at Marble Arch, a blue plaque marks the spot where the original Tyburn Tree stood.

Since 1237, the granting of the "Freedom of the City of London" is one of the oldest surviving traditional ceremonies in Britain.

Origins of the "Freedom" date back to medieval times when groups of craftspeople organised themselves into groups or guilds, which went on to become London's Livery Companies (more about them in a mo).

Over 700 years ago, the City of London regulated that if any livery company wanted to trade within the City, each member or liveryman had to be granted Freedom of the City. London's Freemen had certain trading rights, they were exempt from bridge tolls and were the only members of the City allowed to vote for the Lord Mayor. A voting right which still exists today.

Being a Freeman of London was and still is a highly regarded privilege. Even today, Freedom ceremonies take place inside the Chamberlain's Court on a daily basis. Those who are granted the Freedom of London are given a book entitled *Rules for the Conduct of Life* (perhaps we all need one of those).

Published in 1740 the *Rules for the Conduct of Life* was written by the then Lord Mayor and is still applicable today. Within the publication are a selection of appropriate guidelines for good citizenship and responsible conduct for business and trading activities within the Square Mile.

Rules for THE CONDUCT OF LIFE

Originating over 1,000 years ago, London's Livery Companies are some of the oldest trading associations in Great Britain.

London's Livery Companies represented, regulated and managed the standards of various trades, professions and crafts.

The term livery came from the custom of wearing a "trade" uniform, which is still worn today during official ceremonies.

During medieval times, the liveries operated in a similar way to the crafts guilds. The Masters, who were in charge of the liveries, decided who could officially trade in London and set out the regulations and standards for each given industry.

The livery companies looked after the quality control of the goods they produced, set rates of pay and decided upon employees' working conditions. They managed their own imports and exports and ran their own training apprenticeship schemes.

In return for the trade monopoly they were granted, they looked after their members and their families during sickness and in later life by building almshouses for the elderly, some built schools and many simply made sure their employees had a proper burial.

In 1515, an "order of precedence" was set listing the first 48 livery companies according to their wealth. Today, 108 liveries are in operation and they're still listed in this manner.

If you wander or, better still, take a guided tour through the City of London you may notice street names such as Milk Street, Bread Street, Ironmonger Lane, Poultry, Cloth Fair and Mason's Avenue. Each one marks the site where the trade of some of London's Livery Companies began.

While many of the traditional livery companies are still in operation, those whose trade disappeared during the industrial revolution diversified into a modern-day equivalent.

The Worshipful Company of Horners, London's button makers, moved into the plastics industry. The Worshipful Company of Fan Makers moved into the air-conditioning business (and how cool is that!).

Up until the 1660s each of the livery companies had their own hall, most were destroyed during the Great Fire of London but today 38 Livery Halls still remain.

The term "hallmark" comes from London's Goldsmiths' Hall, the hall of the Worshipful Company of Goldsmiths.

Dating back to a statute laid out by King Edward I in 1327, when the Worshipful Company of Goldsmiths was made responsible for stamping the value and quality of all British gold and silver products – all of which took place at Goldsmiths' hall.

The legacy of London's Livery Companies is very much alive. Many of the companies have and still finance some of Britain's top private schools including Abingdon, Oundle, Charterhouse, Gresham's and Haberdashers'.

The Gunmakers' Company, based at Proof House, is responsible for ensuring that all guns made in the UK are safe to fire.

The Vintners' Company has been responsible for ensuring that EU wine legislation regulations are implemented in Britain through its Wine Standards Board.

The Spectacle Makers' Company is still responsible for the training and examination of the UK's optical technicians.

The Scriveners' Company, connected to the original craft of writing legal documents, still examine, qualify and train professional "Notaries Public" in the City.

By law, all horses must be shod by a registered farrier. The Farriers' Company has a legal duty to set the trade standards and examine those who take a diploma, which entitles them to the formal registration.

Today, London's Livery Companies support their associated industry with prizes, fellowships and scholarships. Some support schools and colleges and many provide almshouses or company pensions.

Many of London's liveries are incredibly wealthy institutions. Their prosperity has been gained over centuries through the acquisition of land and property and in the trading of stocks and shares.

In keeping with their Freemen responsibilities to the City, London's Livery Companies are some of Britain's wealthiest most generous philanthropic organisations, granting millions of pounds to charities and good causes.

For over 2,000 years, London's Square Mile has been the economic powerhouse of Great Britain. It's Europe's largest business district and alongside New York, London is the trading capital of the world.

Home to over 450 different banks, every leading financial institution and a third of the world's largest companies have a headquarters within London's Square Mile. In 2008, income generated by the City's foreign exchange market accounted for 4% of the UK's Gross Domestic Product (GDP).

In June 2011, the London Stock Exchange had a market capitalisation of $3.7495 trillion (that's a million million) making it the fourth largest stock exchange in the world and the largest in Europe. Founded in 1565 by Sir Thomas Gresham, the Royal Exchange was Britain's first-ever commercial trading centre.

The building was inspired by a "bourse" Gresham had seen in Antwerp, a highly organised market with its own trading floor surrounded by shops and offices where traders and merchants could meet to conduct their business.

The Royal Exchange building was destroyed by the Great Fire of London and again in 1838. Today it's a Grade I listed building, which still trades as a shopping centre, home to some of the world's finest brands including De Beers, Tiffany's & Co, Hermes and Penhaligons.

ANNO · ELIZABETHAE · R · XIII · CONDITVM · ANNO · VICTORIAE · R · VIII · RI

JUBILEE WALKWAY

The London Stock Exchange began in 1698 from Jonathan's Coffee House on Change Alley, now Exchange Alley.

It all started when John Casting published *The Course of the Exchange and Other Things* which listed the details of all the different markets, stocks, commodities and futures opportunities.

During the 17th century, London's stockbrokers were not allowed inside the Royal Exchange so they met to discuss deals and investments in the area's coffee shops. About 100 companies sold stocks traded in London, things like cotton, coffee, tea and sugar. Their value fluctuated depending upon international news from London's docks.

The coffee shops employed young boys to meet docking ships and gather news about lost cargoes, large hauls or bumper crops - anything that would affect stock prices. The boys would report back to the coffee shops who charged customers a penny's entrance fee as brokers and potential investors dropped by to find out the financial news of the day.

Over the last 300 years, what began as a twice-weekly publication for company announcements and investors has become a continuous flow of electronic information covering all the different finance and securities markets across the globe.

The London Stock Exchange is based at No. 10 Paternoster Square.

Lloyd's coffee house is famous as the birthplace of Lloyd's of London, the world's oldest insurance company.

It opened around 1688 when owner, Edward Lloyd began catering in coffee and shipping news for London's mariners, merchants and shipowners.

Lloyd's soon became the place where London's shipping industry would get together, talk about the financial risk of their operations and arrange the necessary cover; the Lloyd's insurance market was born.

Today, Lloyd's is based at the Lloyd's Building famously nicknamed the "inside-out building" at No. 1 Lime Street (just look at it). The building designed by Richard Rogers took 33,510 cubic metres of concrete, 30,000 of stainless steel cladding, 12,000 metres of glass and 8 years to build.

The Bank of England was founded in 1694. After the Bank of Sweden, it's the second oldest bank in the world.

The bank was set up at a time when Britain's public finances were in a shoddy state (no change there then!). William Patterson offered a loan to the government of £1.2 million and in return, those who put up the loan could be incorporated as The Governor and Company of the Bank of England.

The first role of the Bank of England was to act as the government's accountant, banker and debt manager. After a while the bank began to finance loans, take deposits and issue banknotes. The bank was nationalised in 1946 and gained independence in 1997.

The Bank of England has been issuing English banknotes for over 300 years. Today's currency is designed and printed by Thomas de la Rue, the oldest currency manufacturer in the world.

De La Rue began trading in London in 1821 when Thomas de la Rue gained a Royal Letters Patent to print playing cards. In 1853 the company was awarded the contract to print Britain's first-ever adhesive, perforated stamps. Then in 1914, on the outbreak of the First World War, the UK treasury commissioned De La Rue to start printing 1- and 10-shilling notes. Today they print the currency for England and another 150 different nations.

In 2011 there was around £52,000,000,000 worth of Bank of England bank notes in circulation. Over £80,000 worth had to be reissued having gone through the UK's washing machines and another £146,000 worth was reissued having been either chewed or eaten (expensive meal). **About 10% have traces of cocaine on them!**

That same year, De La Rue printed over £13,455 million pounds worth of English currency, that's 1,290 million brand new notes - each one printed with its very own traceable serial number (just in case you or your dog decides to eat one).

London's first daily newspaper, *The Daily Courant*, was printed in Fleet Street on the 11th March 1702.

London's printing history began in 1476 when William Caxton installed a printing press in Westminster. In 1500 Wynkyn De Worde (you couldn't write it), one of Caxton's apprentices, was the first printer to open a press on Fleet Street, just opposite Shoe Lane.

Within a few decades, Fleet Street had become home to a number of publishers and printers, primarily supplying print to the four Inns of Court (the professional law association for the barristers of England and Wales), which were (and still are) just up the road.

Within 175 years London's first newspaper arrived.

Fleet Street, famous for being the birthplace of the British newspaper, is named after the River Fleet, London's largest underground river.

As well as printing, Fleet Street was well known for its taverns and coffee houses. Ye Olde Cheshire Cheese pub, which is still open today, was a popular haunt for all kinds of literary types including Ben Jonson, Mark Twain, Charles Dickens and Alfred Tennyson.

Up until the 1980s Fleet Street was synonymous with the British press. It would have been bustling with journalists by day followed by the clattering presses at night. For over 200 years, national and international news organisations have had a headquarters on Fleet Street until the last firm, Reuters, left in 2005.

Today Fleet Street remains home to the Inns of Court and a number of barrister's chambers. Most of today's news corporations have moved to the docklands taking offices in Wapping and Canary Wharf.

With 1.3 million square metres of office space, alongside the City's Square Mile, Canary Wharf is one of the largest financial districts in London.

Canary Wharf was developed as a warehouse as part of what used to be the West India Docks, on the Isle of Dogs. The West India Trading Company owned three of London's largest docks, the first opened in 1802 and the last closed in 1980.

When they were constructed, the West India Docks were the largest purpose-built docks in the world. The docks covered a total area of 295 acres and consisted of a 30-acre Import Dock and a 25-acre Export Dock.

Having two docks, one for incoming and one for outgoing, stopped vessels having to queue for long periods while they waited for others to load or unload. At peak periods, the docks could handle no fewer than 600 vessels at a time.

Concerned primarily with imports from the West Indies, during the 19th century the company looked after the import of rum, molasses, sugar, wines and spirits, coir, jute, spices, coffee and hardwood. By the 20th century and the arrival of refrigeration facilities, they were handling meat, fruit and vegetables and grain.

The size and success of the West India Docks made it a prime target during the Second World War. The raids on Black Saturday, the 7th September 1940 left 430 dead, 1,600 seriously injured and 10,000 homeless. Most of the buildings were destroyed, many never re-opened.

Even though 1961 saw the docks move over 60 million tonnes of cargo, within a decade and the introduction of the shipping container, London's Docklands could no longer compete. Between 1966 and 1976 over 150,000 Londoners lost their jobs. West India closed in 1980.

Between 1981 and March 1998, the London Docklands Development Corporation developed and secured the regeneration plan for London's Docklands. In 1982 the area became an Enterprise Zone offering tax allowances to those who could invest in and develop the area.

In 1987 the Docklands Light Railway and City Airport opened, in 1988 construction for Canary Wharf began and in 1991 the new office developments opened and new tenants moved in.

Dubbed by some as Manhattan-on-Thames, today Canary Wharf is home to some of the tallest skyscrapers in Britain and Europe.

One Canada Square, the tallest building in Canary Wharf has 50 floors and stands at 244 metres above sea level. It was completed in 1991 and up until 2010 it was the tallest building in the United Kingdom and the 15th tallest building in Europe.

The tallest skyscrapers towering over the City of London's skyline include Tower 42 at 183 metres high, Heron Tower at 230 metres and the shortly to be opened Shard London Bridge, which when finished will be over 310 metres tall.

Tower 42, formerly known as the NatWest Tower, was completed in 1980 and until the completion of the Heron Tower, it was the tallest building in the City for over three decades.

Heron Tower, 110 Bishopsgate, which opened in March 2011, is home to the largest privately owned aquarium in Europe. The 70,000-litre tank is 12 metres wide, 4 metres high and 2 metres long and has over 1,200 inhabitants.

At 180 metres tall, one of the City's landmark skyscrapers has been lovingly nicknamed the Gherkin.

The Gherkin or as it's officially known, 30 St Mary's Axe, was designed by Norman Foster and Partners and opened in 2004. When it was put on the market in 2006, the building sold for £630 million, the most expensive office block of its time.

London Bridge marks the site of the oldest bridge in London; the spot where London's first inhabitants would have crossed the Thames and made landfall in Londinium.

The first London Bridge, constructed around 50AD, would have been made of wood. The first stone bridge took 33 years to build and was completed by 1209.

In 1305, London Bridge became home to the severed heads of traitors who'd been sentenced to execution by the Old Bailey. The head of William Wallace was the first to be spiked outside the gatehouse, starting a tradition that went on for over 355 years.

The next London Bridge was designed by Sir John Rennie and made from Haytor granite (chipped and shipped all the way from Devon). Rennie's bridge cost a total of £2.5 million to construct (about £185 million in today's money) and opened in 1831.

By 1896, with over 8,000 people crossing ever hour, Rennie's London Bridge was believed to be the busiest place in London.

The London Bridge that crosses the Thames today was opened in 1973 by Her Majesty the Queen and Sir John Rennie's bridge relocated to Lake Havasu City, Arizona.

No joke, such was the uproar at demolishing Rennie's bridge that an American business put up the money to have the old bridge dismantled and shipped to the US. It arrived in on the 5th July 1968 and opened in 1971. The story goes that they thought they were getting Tower Bridge! Anyway, today it's a popular tourist attraction.

Between Kew and Tower Bridge, there are 24 bridges spanning the Thames.

The City of London has five bridges: Tower Bridge, London Bridge, Blackfriars Bridge, Southwark Bridge and the Millennium Bridge. Each of which are maintained by funding from The Bridge House Estate, a charitable trust set up in 1282, which is managed by the City of London Corporation.

In years gone by, anyone crossing one of London's bridges would have had to pay a fee. Bridge House collected those fees for the City and over the centuries the charity became substantially wealthy.

As funds from bridge tolls and property rental on the bridges grew, Bridge House invested in land and property throughout the City. Over the centuries, the Estate has acquired a significant portfolio, which generates over £35 million in rental income each year.

Today, Bridge House Estate is estimated to have funds over £500 million in its coffers but if any of the City's five bridges collapsed or need maintenance or replacing, the reconstruction bill would be paid for by Bridge House, not by the government or any other public body.

When Tower Bridge opened in 1894 it was the most sophisticated bridge in the world. What made it unique was its "bascule" or "see-saw" steam-powered hydraulic system, which enabled the bridge to open allowing large ships along the Thames.

Tower bridge was designed by Horace Jones, it took 432 workmen 8 years to build the structure which was made from 11,000 tonnes of steel. Today over 40,000 vehicles cross the bridge and it opens to river traffic over 900 times a year (go on, just put your foot down, I'm sure you'll make it).

With over 54,000 vehicles travelling over it, Blackfriars Bridge is the busiest bridge in the city and Southwark Bridge is one of the quietest with just 17,000 vehicles a day.

The London Millennium Footbridge, famously nicknamed the wobbly bridge, is the first footbridge to be built over the Thames for more than a century.

The design for the bridge, which is a stainless steel suspension bridge, came from a design competition won by Arup, Foster and Partners and Sir Anthony Caro.

Within two days of the bridge opening in June 2000, a group of walkers crossing the bridge on a fund-raising effort for Save the Children noticed a rather wobbly swaying motion and the "wobbly bridge" as it became known had to be closed for modifications.

The new, not so wobbly bridge opened again in 2002 and today's structure can support a total of 5,000 pedestrians across the Thames at anyone time.

The River Thames is estimated to be about 58 million years old.

At 210 miles long, it's the longest river in England and, after the River Severn, it's the 2nd longest river in the UK.

For over two millennia the River Thames has been the lifeblood of London. The banks of the River Thames have provided port and safe harbour to hundreds of thousands of ships and seafarers making the Port of London one of the busiest ports in the world.

The first Port of London was built during the first century by the Romans. The Pool of London as it became known ran from London Bridge to Tower Bridge with "lower pool" extending from Tower Bridge down to Cherry Garden Pier, Rotherhithe.

During the 1700s and 1800s, London Port had a total of 18 kilometres (11 miles) of wooden wharves along the Thames and some 1,500 cranes, which could load and unload over 60,000 ships each year.

The explosion of overseas trading created hundreds of new jobs. People from all over Britain and abroad flocked to London's dockyards for jobs as lightermen.

London's lightermen moved cargo between the ships and the stores in their lighter boats. London's watermen moved people!

In 1851 the borough of West Ham was recorded as having 19,000 residents, by 1901 it had 270,000 due to the enormous labour force created by the docks.

The Port of London Authority (PLA) was formed on the 31st March 1909 with the aim of bringing order to the chaos that ran along the banks of the River Thames.

At its peak in the 1930s, the PLA looked after 713 acres of dock water (that's 2,506 Olympic swimming pools). London's docklands spread over 5 areas and had 47 basins and a total quayside that ran for 36 miles (or the same distance as Charing Cross to Southend!).

In its first year of operation, the PLA managed 18.6 million tonnes of import and export cargo. Half a century on and it handles somewhere in the region of 61.3 million tonnes each year.

Today most of London's cargo is managed at Purfleet and Tilbury by private companies and the PLA looks after the safety and navigation of ships and the many Thames leisure users.

The River Thames is believed to take its name from the Sanskrit word "tamas" meaning dark. Others believe the river was named after the Roman word "Tamesis" or "Thamesis" which originated from the word "tam" meaning wide and "isis" meaning water.

Flowing 201 miles from its source, a small stream at Kemble in the Cotswold Hills, Gloucestershire, the Thames journeys eastwards through Oxford, Windsor and across Greater London before reaching its mouth in the North Sea at Southend in Essex.

The Thames is both a tidal and non-tidal waterway. The tidal part, known as the Tideway, flows inland for 160 kilometres (that's 90 miles) from Southend until Teddington Lock, near Richmond, West London.

The Tideway sees water levels rise and fall twice a day and depending on the time of year, the height of the tidal part of the river can increase by up to 7 metres (that's 24 feet, the height of your average house!). Tide heights and times for the Thames in London are measured at London Bridge.

Because of the sheer size and tidal/non-tidal nature of the River Thames, large parts of London are prone to flooding...

... On the 7th January 1928, London experienced the most devastating flood the capital had ever seen.

Heavy snow, then a sharp thaw at the source of the Thames doubled the amount of water flowing down the river.

Heavy rain, a high spring tide and a storm surge out in the North Sea increased the amount of water entering at the mouth of the river. Water levels at Southend were recorded to be 1.5 metres higher than normal.

Recent dredging, deepening the Thames for cargo vessels, meant there was a deeper channel for water to travel from the sea in the direction of London.

Water poured over the embankment, the Chelsea embankment collapsed. Westminster and the House of Commons were damaged and the Tate Gallery saw between 8 and 15 feet of floodwater in its lower galleries.

Even the moat at the Tower of London, which had been empty for 80 years, was refilled with floodwater.

The highest water levels ever recorded in London were taken on 7th January 1928 at 1.30am. The Thames had swollen to over 5.5 metres (that's 18 feet) higher than the normal datum line.

The Thames flood of 1928 claimed the lives of 14 people and made a further 4,000 homeless. Millbank had to be almost entirely rebuilt (which gave us the new MI5 building - top secret so don't tell anyone!) **Lambeth Bridge was completely replaced and the height of the Embankment was raised.**

During the rebuild, plans for a Thames Barrier were put forward but rejected on the grounds that many believed a barrier would affect the trade traffic getting in and out of the Port of London. However, another 25 years and another severe flood later, which this time claimed the lives of 307 Britons, soon put plans for the Thames Barrier back on the bill.

The North Sea floods of 1953 were the worst flooding disaster the UK has ever seen.

Areas in Essex, Suffolk and Lincolnshire were affected as well as communities in Belgium and Holland. In Britain 307 people lost their lives to the flood, 30,000 people had to be evacuated and 24,000 homes were damaged.

Along the Thames estuary, Canvey Island, one of the river's 80 islands, was completely devastated. Lying just 2 feet above sea level, the floodwater at Canvey claimed the lives of 58 residents and 13,000 local people had to be temporarily evacuated.

If the North Sea surge of 1953 had continued into London, the death toll would have been even higher and the clean up operation would have been colossal.

Plans for a Thames Barrier were taken much more seriously and a report, written by Sir Herman Bondi, determined that a flood barrier with moveable gates was the best solution.

Today, the Thames Barrier is one of the largest moveable flood barriers on the planet. It is made up of ten 3,300-tonne steel gates, which span 520 metres of the Thames near Woolwich.

The gates protect 125 square kilometres of Central London from flooding. When raised, the gates are as high as a 5-storey building and as wide as the opening of Tower Bridge!

1.5 million people live within London's tidal flood zone; without the barrier 35,000 homes would be at risk as well as the Dome, Canary Wharf, City Hall, the Globe Theatre, the Tate Modern, the London Eye and the Houses of Parliament.

The Thames Barrier took eight years to build and went into operation in 1983. The project cost £535 million (around £2 billion in today's money) and requires a further £8 million a year to operate.

Since opening, the gates of the Thames Barrier have been raised over 411 times. In its 25-year lifespan, the barrier is estimated to have saved London from flooding over 70 times.

When I think of London I think of, and very much feel, its might, not its vulnerability.

London has stature. It has elegance, grace and above all resilience but not when it comes to Old Father Thames and the force of Mother Nature. No, despite its grandeur, London is not without its frailty.

The Thames has been the lifeblood of London for centuries; the capital's aorta revitalising the city with cargos and characters from all over the world.

To me there is always something very special about a place that has water running through it (or indeed up to it). Whether it's the low or the high of a tide or the rise and fall of a riverbank, water gives us life and it reminds us of life. It changes the scenery and it puts us in touch with the mercy of nature. Tides giveth and they taketh away.

As the MP John Burns once put it, "the Thames is liquid history". For me it's been liquid gold. The trade and travellers that sailed their way into the Port of London have given the city its colourful character and all manner of commodities that still, thousands of years on, make London the trading capital of the world.

For many of us that's all London is – the capital of UK trade, the nerve centre of Great Britain. The "big smoke" where all the big bosses work, where all the big bunce gets earned and where all the big bully-boy politicians get decisions made. I hope this book has illustrated that there is much more to London than that.

Despite our own rural cynicism about centralised decision making, fat-cat salaries and the haughty political performances that play out on *Westminster Live*, we love London. As we put this book together, we were reminded of the much bigger and symbolic role our beloved capital had played in our lives.

We lovingly remembered the brilliant school trips we had. Our first trip on a coach or a train as we visited the Natural History Museum, the Science Museum and the many great London galleries (there wasn't the London Eye back then).

For most British schoolchildren a trip to London was, and still is, one of those life affirming rites of passage. When I first went to London I felt like I'd had some kind of initiation, a coming of age, as though somehow, because I'd visited London - was a grown up.

As we painstakingly laid up the text on the theatre and venue pages, we remembered those special birthday treats where our parents, carers or teachers took us to see a London show, a special West End pantomime or a full-on concert or a sporting event.

We talked about the commute we once had when we'd got our first proper job.

We talked about wild nights out or special dinner dates.

Above all, we each recounted a seemingly endless night out, whether as an adult or a child, when life "up town" felt so expansive, when being there gave us the sense that we were in a place where everything and anything was possible – a city of dreams and a city that never sleeps.

No wonder! Look at it. London is so diverse and so culturally rich. It's got intimate villages and lush green parks. It's got elegant crescents and enormous skyscrapers. It's got seedy bits and swanky bits. It's so old and yet so young. It's so fast and happening and yet so anciently established.

There's a great quote; "when a man is tired of London, he is tired of life". I would say, "when a man (or woman actually!) is fired by London he (or she) is fired with life". That's how I feel when I go there.

London is big, it's beautiful, it's been beaten and burned – it's got some pretty brutal parts to it and some pretty bruised places too – but hey, it's a city that's bright and has never been belittled.

London is a great place and a key ingredient in the Great of Great Britain. We hope you've enjoyed a little taste of it here.

Contributors and references

Bibliography:

London Lore, Steven Stroud,
Arrow Books, 2010.

Secret London, Andrew Duncan,
New Holland Publishers, 2009.

I never knew that about London,
Christopher Winn, Ebury Press, 2007.

Not for Parents London,
Lonely Planet, 2011.

Waldorf 100 years, The Waldorf Hotel, 2008.

The Book of London Lists, Nick Rennison,
Canongate, 2006.

*A Profile of Londoners by Country of
Birth*, the Greater London Authority.

Leading to a greener London,
the Greater London Authority.

Sources:

Barts and the London NHS Trust –
www.bartsandthelondon.nhs.uk

Battersea Dogs and Cats Home –
www.battersea.org.uk

BBC News – www.news.bbc.co.uk

Bevis Marks – www.bevismarks.org.uk

Big Ben – www.bigbenfacts.co.uk

British Transport Police –
www.btp.police.uk

Claridge's Hotel – www.claridges.co.uk

End Child Poverty –
www.endchildpoverty.org.uk

Exploring 20th Century London –
www.20thcenturylondon.org.uk

Fortnum and Mason –
www.fortnumandmason.com

Fuller's Brewery – www.fullers.co.uk

Harrods – www.harrods.com

Harvey Nichols – www.harveynichols.com

Historic Royal Palaces – www.hrp.org.uk

HMV – www.hmv.com

Imperial War Museum – www.iwm.org.uk

Kettner's Restaurant & Champagne Bar –
www.kettners.com

Liberty – www.liberty.com

London 2012 – www.london2012.com

London Councils –
www.londoncouncils.gov.uk

London for Free – www.londonforfree.net

**London Skills and Employment
Observatory** – www.lseo.org.uk

London's Chinatown –
www.chinatown-london.org.uk

M. Manze – www.manze.co.uk

Madame Tussaud's –
www.madametussauds.com

Marks and Spencer –
www.marksandspencer.com

Metropolitan Police – www.met.police.uk

Metropolitan Police Historical Archives –
www.met.police.uk/history/archives.htm

New Covent Garden Market –
www.newcoventgardenmarket.com

Office for National Statistics –
www.ons.gov.uk

RFU – www.rfu.com

Rigby and Peller – www.rigbyandpeller.com

Ronnie Scott's – www.ronniescotts.co.uk

Royal Mail and Post Office Counters –
www.royalmail.com

Royal Parks – www.royalparks.org.uk

Rules Restaurant – www.rules.co.uk

Selfridges – www.selfridges.com

Simpson's-in-the-Strand –
www.simpsonsinthestrand.co.uk

Simpson's Tavern –
www.simpsonstavern.co.uk

St Mary-Le-Bow – www.stmarylebow.co.uk

St Paul's Cathedral – www.st-pauls.co.uk

Sweetings Fish Restaurant –
www.sweetingsrestaurant.com

The Barbican – www.barbican.org.uk

The British Library – www.bl.uk

The British Museum –
www.britishmuseum.org

The London Central Mosque –
www.iccuk.org

The City of London –
www.cityoflondon.gov.uk

The Dorchester – www.thedorchester.com

The Environment Agency –
www.environment-agency.gov.uk

The Geographers' Maps Company –
www.az.co.uk

The Globe Theatre –
www.shakespearesglobe.com

The Grosvenor Hotel – www.guoman.com

The Guardian – www.guardian.co.uk

The Houses of Parliament –
www.parliament.uk

The Independent – www.independent.co.uk

The Knowledge – www.the-knowledge.org

The Lanesborough Hotel –
www.thelanesborough.com

The Langham Hotel –
www.london.langhamhotels.co.uk

The London Borough – www.bromley.gov.uk

The London Development Agency –
www.lda.gov.uk

The London Drum – www.londondrum.com

The London Eye – www.londoneye.com

The London Fire Brigade –
www.london-fire.gov.uk

The London Marathon –
www.virginlondonmarathon.com

The London Symphony Orchestra –
www.lso.co.uk

The London Vintage Taxi Association –
www.lvta.co.uk

The National Gallery –
www.nationalgallery.org.uk

The National Portrait Gallery –
www.npg.org.uk

The National Theatre –
www.nationaltheatre.org.uk

The Natural History Museum –
www.nhm.ac.uk

The Pearly Story –
www.cockneymuseum.u-net.com

The Ritz London – www.theritzlondon.com

The Royal Albert Hall –
www.royalalberthall.com

The Royal Festival Hall –
www.thesouthbankcentre.co.uk

The Royal Opera House – www.roh.org.uk

The Royal Philharmonic Orchestra –
www.rpo.co.uk

The Savoy – www.fairmont.com/savoy

The Science Museum –
www.sciencemuseum.org.uk

The Tate – www.tate.org.uk

The Telegraph – www.telegraph.co.uk

The Victoria and Albert Museum –
www.vam.ac.uk

The Waldorf Hilton Hotel –
www.waldorfhilton.co.uk

This is London – www.thisislondon.co.uk

This is Money – www.thismoney.co.uk

Transport for London – www.tfl.gov.uk

Twentieth Century London –
www.20thcenturylondon.org.uk

Victorian Fortune City –
www.victorian.fortunecity.com

Visit London – www.visitlondon.com

Visit the city – www.visitthecity.co.uk

Wembley Stadium –
www.wembleystadium.com

Westminster City Council –
www.westminster.gov.uk

Westminster Abbey –
www.westminster-abbey.org

Wimbledon Lawn Tennis Club –
www.wimbledon.com

Photo credits:

Thank you to Shutterstock image library and the following:

Pages 1 & 2 – EDF London Eye.
Page 6 – The M25, Idle Format.
Page 8 – HMV Oxford Street, HMV.
Page 11 – Manze's Pie Shop, the Manze family.
Page 14 – Aerial View of London, Lars Ploughman.
Page 25 – Container City, Martin Pearce.
Page 28 – Battersea Cats and Dogs Home.
Page 47 – Carnaby Street, Getty Images.
Page 49 – EMI and The Beatles, Getty Images.
Page 65 – Joseph Bazelgette, Getty Images.
Page 68 – The Wombles, Getty Images.
Page 72 – Liverpool Street, James Mitchell.
Page 78 – The George Inn, the National Trust.
Page 81 – The Savoy Hotel, Justin Goring.
Page 86 – The Waldorf tea dance, the Waldorf Hotel.
Page 96 – The EDF London Eye, EDF London Eye.
Page 98 – Crystal Palace, Getty Images.
Page 122 – Kensington Palace, Maxwell Hamilton.
Page 142 – H.M. Queen, The Press Association.
Page 144 – The Gold Coach, Getty Images.
Page 146 – House in Fulham, Getty Images.
Page 150 – Covent Garden, Getty Images.
Page 152 – Covent Garden Station, Tom Pagenet.
Pages 168 & 169 – White Horse Final, Getty Images.
Pages 170 & 171 – Wembley Stadium, David Jones.
Page 181 – Hyde Park, Garry Knight.
Pages 184 & 185 – The Thames, Getty Images.
Page 187 – The Olympic Stadium, London 2012.
Pages 192 & 193 – UK from space, NASA.
Page 200 – Beigel Bake, Tom Barnecutt.
Page 204 – Ronnie Scott, Ronnie Scott's.
Page 208 – Empire Windrush, Getty Images.
Page 213 – Notting Hill Carnival, Valters Krontals.
Page 217 – Costermongers, Getty Images.
Page 218 – Pearly Kings and Queens, Garry Knight.
Page 229 – Traffic jam in the 1960s, David Fowler.
Page 237 – Hyde Park, Getty Images.
Page 242 – Trafalgar Square, Museum of London.
Pages 246 & 247 – Smog, Getty Images.
Page 255 – Routemaster on Service J, Arriva.
Page 275 – St Paul's Cathedral, Getty Images.
Page 293 – Conduct of Life, Paul Colledge.
Page 314 – London Bridge, Cornell University.
Page 325 – London in 1928 floods, Getty Images.

Thanks:

I'd like to dedicate this book to a few of my mates who I have shared wonderful times with, both in London and in Cornwall; Tom Barnecutt, who has just left his homeland in Cornwall for the Big Smoke, Janine Fahri and Bryher Scudamore, two inspirational women who I don't see often enough. A big up to all my buddies from Essex (it is the only way) and all the great times we had in Matt's, Spud's and Rachel's extraordinary house in Aslett Road, Earlsfield (remember the sixties night and the stretched limo!). Thanks as always to my wonderful and very patient designer Paul Colledge, editor and wordsmith David Meneer, proofreader Martin Bates, journalist Stuart James (for the sporty bit) and my print buyer Mark Robinson at Webmart. Thank you to Bill at Central Books and Bunnie and Adam at Heritage Books. Thank you to my family and friends in Cornwall for their continuous support as the Lovely Little Book collection expands and finally a big thank you to all of the individuals and organisations who have contributed images.

The index refers to the text only - not photos.
Index entries refer to page numbers. Entries
are in letter-by-letter alphabetical order.